ORIGINS OF THE SACRED

Anne Bancroft spent the early part of her life in the Quaker village of Jordans. While her four children were growing up she became a lecturer in Comparative Religion, and at the same time began her own quest for spiritual understanding. Over the years she has found strength and inspiration in Buddhism and a deepening understanding of western mysticism. She is the author of several other books on religion and mysticism.

ANNE BANCROFT

ORIGINS OF THE SACRED

THE WAY OF THE SACRED IN WESTERN TRADITION

ARKANA
LONDON AND NEW YORK

First published in 1987
by ARKANA PAPERBACKS
ARKANA PAPERBACKS is an imprint of
Routledge & Kegan Paul Ltd

11 New Fetter Lane, London EC4P 4EE

Published in the USA by
Routledge & Kegan Paul Inc.
in association with Methuen Inc.
29 West 35th Street, New York, NY 10001

Set in Sabon, 10 on 11 pt
by Inforum Ltd, Portsmouth
and printed in Great Britain
by The Guernsey Press Co. Ltd,
Guernsey, Channel Islands

Library of Congress Cataloging in Publication Data

Bancroft, Anne, 1923–
Origins of the Sacred.

Bibliography: p.
Includes index.
1. Religion—History. I. Title.
BL48.B362 1987 291'.09 86–24786

British Library CIP Data also available

ISBN 1–85063–028–3

CONTENTS

Acknowledgment

The author and publisher would like to thank E. Duckett and Collins Publishers for permission to quote a verse from *The Wondering Saints* (1959).

Introduction

There are certain revelations which come to us from the timeless, non-historical world of myth. They express what has always been true, and what remains true today. They transcend the limitations of formal religion for they are not bounded by historical events, personages or scriptures; yet they enlighten because they reveal the timeless realisations going on within man always.

This book is about such events and the ways in which they have been expressed in the history and prehistory of western Europe. The knowledge of a higher dimension of existence has never been easy to explain or describe. It is connected with certain experiences so subtle that there is nothing to which they can be compared; and at the same time so real that they seem more real than ordinary sense experiences. In the end, they can only be hinted at by means of symbols. Such symbols arose with the early mind of mankind and are with us still today.

Language is the first and greatest of these symbols. With language humanity was born, for each word denoted an experience common to all and creatively called into being.

> Each word originally was a focus of energies, in which the transformations of reality into the vibrations of the human voice – the vital expression of the human soul – took place. Through these vocal creations man took possession of the world – and more than that: he discovered a new dimension, a world within himself, opening upon the vista of a higher form of life. . .[72]

From the evidence of history it seems that mankind's desire has always been to be in contact with his spirit. He has forever tried to reach out beyond the boundaries of his senses and to find the divine, in whatever period of time. Using the symbols which were apparent to him, he labelled his ideals as appropriately as he could, usually as gods and goddesses; and yet always with the knowledge that behind the symbol lay the mystery of Reality.

By way of such representations as supreme deities and lesser ones, ancestors and spirits, humans were able to reach a sense of otherness and transcendence upon which life and being could be grounded. The great mysteries of birth, death and rebirth came to contain meaning and significance beyond the human because of the immanence of the divine felt to be present in the physical universe. The object – the beech tree or the grey sea – as it appeared in ordinary sense-experience, pointed to a reality which was not contained within that experience but was boundless. The ultimate meaning to which it led was not fully reachable by the senses but every sense object was like a pointing finger showing the way to the reality behind the appearance. The whole of the universe was infused with the sacred, containing an aspect which transcended the finite and made it immeasurable.

It is one of the tragedies of modern western religion that it has divorced itself from its myths and relies only on its history, which makes the living deity into an abstract. Once, though, the great human experiences were based on cosmic myths which operated in sacred time and space. They implied a deep sense of relationship with nature. The physical formations of rocks, trees, rivers and hills were luminous with meaning. The material world was seen as alive and beautiful and providing a sacred arena for human beings and their activities.

In such a climate everything was symbolised, so that it pointed beyond itself to a greater truth. But now we have removed the spiritual from nature, placing it far away in an abstract 'God', and in its place we have invented new deities – science, technology and our physical well-being. And because we no longer see any part of nature or any condition of it as sacred, we poison all its resources. In so doing we have become discontented and unhappy, feeling ourselves to be alien in a senseless world.

Life has never been easy at any time. Yet once it was rich and full of meaning *for many more people* because it was alive with being. The possibility of a direct experience with the divine at many levels was there and gave significance to impressions that have become meaningless or trivial today – 'for what is real and true look at these stones, this bread, this spring of water, these sea-waves, the horizon with its pure, untroubled line. Only perceive purely and the spiritual and the material vibrate as one.'[123]

Such a direct intuition of the numinous disappeared for many westerners some 2000 years ago, for:

> no longer could spirit be seen-beheld in stones, waters, springs, trees, groves, animals – and eventually not even in human beings. Instead, spirit became an ethical abstraction . . . the living out of the myth was terminated by separating the human from the divine. Dogmatism was substituted for conscious myth-making. . . Faith was no longer *pistis* ('trust in one's own experience') but henceforth blind acceptance, divorced from subjective personal experience.[170]

Yet we should not despair. For this century has seen a new growth in the spirit with the spread of eastern religions to the west, reminding the west of its own mysticism; and it is apparent that men and women are still searching for transcendent insight and for true values to live by. The Mystery has reasserted itself and the great questions which were the basis for all the religions – what is life and what is death – are being asked again. But now we also ask how we can become whole, living in honesty and love, and these are perhaps the most religious questions of all.

In the quest for insight it may be useful to look at the particularities of different ages as they stand out from their vast conditioning background – the spirit of Neanderthal man within the Ice Age; the deep reverence for the shaman as depicted in cave paintings; the great Mother Goddess who was worshipped throughout Europe and beyond while the seas were forming round our coasts; the identity of the spirit with the earth itself as shown in passage-graves and stone circles; sun and moon worship and alignment to the stars; the coming of the Celts and their understanding of reincarnation; the Roman conquerors who brought with them the mystery cults; the dark religion and magic of the Anglo-Saxons; the coming of the Christians; the fearsome invasions of the Vikings and the power of the northern gods; and finally, against a background of war, plague and persecution, the teachings of the mystics of the Church.

To look at our religious roots and to see the ways in which other humans at different times have asked the same questions as we ask – and what they have found – that is what this book is about.

CHAPTER ONE
Early consciousness: the dream time

The minds of the very earliest human beings would have received an imprint of the landscape they inhabited, that of the cave and forest, ocean and mountain; and this primary imprint with its wonders and signs would have become the ground of the mind itself, never leaving humanity until supplanted by city street. Even today the imprint still affects us, creating longings for the countryside and for wildness. We sense the mystery of the universe itself in solitude and unspoilt surroundings. And indeed that basic sense of an infinite mystery at the root of all life would have been there for our ancestors as it is for us. For they knew that they came from mystery into the world and left it again for that same mystery. The formulation of doctrines and creeds and the many purposes of gods or a God were unlikely to have been part of their life but we would do them an injustice were we to consider that they would not have been as capable as we are, if not more so, of entering into the heart of existence and feeling its infinite levels of reality.

Historians who pronounce on the religions of early man tend to see our prehistoric ancestors as fearful, awestruck and bewildered by the harshness of existence, and given to inventing gods, demons and spirits whom they could appease by ritual and sacrifice. This superstitious aspect of religion was no doubt important to them – as it still is to us today when we touch wood to prevent bad luck – but to limit their spiritual capacity to this side of religion alone is to misjudge the whole nature of the life of the spirit. For it is apparent that from the very beginning of human existence men and women have struggled to know the full reality of life, to reach beyond themselves and to aspire to the unknown. And this search for the spiritual did not arise from merely a life of food-gathering and hunting. Somehow it was awakened in mankind, drawing him upwards. Many might call it the urge to find God which was initiated by God. Another way of looking at it, the non-theistic way, is put by Alan Watts:

> Human beings are aware of a world because, and only because, it is the sort of world that breeds knowing organisms. Humanity is not one thing and the world another; it has always been difficult for us to see that any organism is so embedded in its environment that the evolution of so complex and intelligent a creature as man could never have come to pass without a reciprocal evolution of the environment. An intelligent man argues, without any resort to supernaturalism, an intelligent universe.[166]

That the universe itself is intelligent may sound like fantasy, yet the findings of modern physics bear this out: the eminent physicist David Bohm believes that consciousness is not distinct from matter, and that both are aspects of a creative and dynamic 'implicate order' which is enfolded into the universe itself.[20]

Perhaps we could say that the nature of the universe is also the nature of that which transcends us, and through the raising of our consciousness we come to know this for ourselves. The dawn of such awareness must have arisen with man's sense of himself, his self-consciousness. And although this was not recorded in ways that we can understand, to doubt that men and women had that experience is to mistake the ways of the spirit altogether.

It has recently been discovered that developed humans lived in Europe much earlier than had previously been thought. A new amino-acid dating technique is beginning to improve our knowledge about the climatic fluctuations during the Ice Ages and the consequent movements of people. The ancient beach deposits on the coast of Sussex, thirty metres above sea level, are half a million years old. Well-formed hand axes have been found there. If they turn out to be equally old it will show that early man was in Britain at that time – long before he was thought to be. So our quest, which starts in one of the oldest inhabited caves in Europe, may relate to an immense age past.

Kent's Cavern, on the south Devon coast, opens out on to a hillside which overlooks a tree-filled combe leading to the sea. It is an idyllic site today. When it was first lived in by our ancestors it would have looked on to great areas of forest, for Britain was then part of the land mass of Europe and neither the Channel nor the North Sea existed. The first great Ice Age had receded, the second was yet to come.

In this interglacial period the weather would have been ideal – the sort we dream of in our cold winters today. Warm but not too hot; a climate which could support such animals as the sabre-toothed tiger, the great cave lion and massive cave bear, rhinoceros, hippopotamus, hyena and elephant.

Our early ancestors were mainly vegetarians, living on roots and berries. The pear-shaped flint tools found in Kent's Cavern were more likely to have been used for digging up roots than for clubbing animals. In small groups they would have sought out the most fertile regions where roots, shoots, nuts, berries and fruit could be gathered. If we could only recover their vocabulary[42] we may be sure it would reflect an accurate and intimate knowledge of the plant world. For hundreds of thousands of years, wild fruit and vegetable, nut and berry supplemented the occasional meat which was the food of early humans. Probably insects too would have been part of the diet, as well as grubs and snails.

The cave itself is immense, some three and a half acres. A thousand yards of passages and galleries have been opened up to the public with electric lighting, so it is possible to wander deep inside and feel on one's skin the even temperature which never varies from 52° Fahrenheit. Since the cave is hollowed out of limestone, it is porous and the musical planging of water is always present. The pleasing power of the sound is especially felt when the lights are turned out and total velvety blackness – a blackness more profound than any night – engulfs one like the womb. Here too, revealed by the light, are great chambers of multi-coloured rock, mainly the red of iron and green of copper, showing a glowing beauty undreamed of when one stands outside. Stalactites and stalagmites descend and rise, sometimes melting into one another to form strange convoluted 'candles'. Small groups of stalagmites rise up in grottoes like miniature towns, while the glistening icicle-like stalactites solidify to form cascading surfaces like polished jade.

Nothing feels inimical or hostile in the warmth of the cave. It is at the same time both majestic and intimate. So it is not difficult to imagine such a place, consistently mild and excellently ventilated, a cosy home to many stray creatures including some of the earliest humans.

For those very first men and women, heightened perception of their surroundings would probably have constituted their basic sense of religion. They were unlikely to have separated themselves from the environment in the way we do today. Like the trees of the forests they were as they were, and their sense of spiritual life would have come perhaps from their openness to what was there – the streams bubbling up through the ground, the curve of the hills, the clouds. This is the beginning of all mystical experience, well testified to by mystics throughout the ages.

For an immense aeon these people existed in a timeless world – we know this because they continued to use the same primitive stone tools for some 400,000 years. In this timeless 'dream' period they probably lived very much in the present, were open and receptive, and were not tormented by desire for 'things'. We might have found them no more primitive than ourselves in their morals and modes of thought, for the ability to make machines is not the measure of culture and goodness.

It is probable that the tools they used were charged with 'a certain sacrality'.[58] All the great discoveries of mankind – the use of stone and wood for housing and weapons, the learning of fire-making, and the wheel – were not only means of survival but were also the creative ground for religious myth. Many beliefs and mythologies have arisen around tools and implements and we should never forget all that they *cannot* tell us. For every object on its own, even in our own time, loses its significance when it cannot be set into a system of meanings. So, too, the flint axes must have held a much greater significance for their culture than we can ever know.[63]

THE WORLD OF THE NEANDERTHALS

These groups of people did not die out during the next era of time so much as become added to by others. The change between 250,000 BCE and 100,000 BCE was not dramatic. But then, somewhere between 120,000 BCE and 100,000 BCE a strange new race emerged – the Neanderthals – so named because their remains were found in the Neander valley in Germany.

Neanderthal man was what we usually see depicted in comics as the Stone Age caveman. He had a low receding forehead coming down to jutting bony brows. His upper jaw was huge, his chin missing altogether. His head hung forward from his spine and he was clumsily made, short and strong, although these physical characteristics varied greatly from one group to another. Some historians believe that he was an adaptation to Arctic conditions and that his type disappeared when those conditions passed away. Whatever the reasons, his was a particular race which lasted until about 40,000 BCE, when it appears to have died out. It is thought, however, that rather than becoming extinct there was considerable interbreeding between the Neanderthals and the more modern races with whom he shared the planet for some twenty thousand years towards the end of his era, so that his characteristics were gradually absorbed into the mainstream of mankind. Nevertheless, many of the more extraordinary Neanderthal skulls are from later rather than earlier individuals, showing that he was a recent as well as a primitive type.

> We know from the size of his brain that his intellectual capacity . . . was not innately different from modern man's. And this is often said. Yet it obscures rather than illuminates the difference between them and us. From what we can infer from the very primitive people who still exist . . . early man had no sense of time, no concern with the past or future. Perhaps, as for the Australian aborigine, all but the present was the 'dream-time'. Furthermore there was nothing in the pattern of his economic or social activity to drive him to think otherwise. Consciousness of the historical process is one of the most remarkable features of civilised existence, but its emergence as a factor in the intellectual life of man has been exceptionally slow.[137]

In her perceptive novel *The Clan of the Cave Bear*, Jean Auel suggests that:

> All those primitive people, with almost no frontal lobes and speech limited by undeveloped vocal organs, but with huge brains – larger than those of any race of man then living or future generations yet unborn – were unique. They were the culmination of a branch of mankind whose brain was developed in the back of their heads, in the occipital and parietal that controls vision and bodily sensations and stores memory.

> And their memory made them extraordinary. In them the unconscious knowledge of ancestral behaviour called instinct had evolved. Stored in the back of their large brains were not just their own memories, but the memories of their forebears. They . . . could not conceive a future any different from the past, could not devise innovative alternatives for tomorrow. All their knowledge, everything they did was a repetition of something that had been done before. Even storing food for seasonal changes was the result of past experience.[7]

Neanderthal man has remained an enigma to researchers although a great deal has been discovered about him. He inhabited large areas of the world and it is thought he was alive in North Africa until 30,000 BCE. But suddenly he was gone, disappeared altogether, his caves abandoned and his culture over.

We now know that he had a strong religious sense, that he had awakened to the mystery of death and that he believed in an afterlife – thus forever removing humankind from the realm of animals. He buried bodies in specially dug graves, sometimes putting stones around the body to protect it from the pressure of the earth. The graves were usually dug within caves that were used by the living for homes, and often were close to a hearth as if fire was part of the ritual attending death. Tools of bone or stone and joints of meat were buried with the body, showing a strong belief in an afterlife. A young man buried in France was laid on a pillow of flints and a fine flint axe was placed in readiness by his hand, while in Iraq a body was surrounded by flowers and medicinal herbs. Indeed, if we look at burial customs today, there does not seem to be a great gap but more a continuous expression of custom which has come down from at least 100,000 years ago. Very often such graves were pointed in an east-west direction, with the head at the east so that the rising sun would enter the corpse's eyes and wake him to new life, as it did for living sleepers. Even when arranged on his side with his knees drawn up, the body was still placed to see the early morning light with its eyes. The common position for a body was that of the foetus in the womb and so it would seem that:

a new birth was believed to take place – probably in this world rather than another.

Corpses were covered with red ochre, the colour of blood. From primitive peoples today, we know that this reassures the dead that they will have 'breath, warmth and life'. The historian Ivar Lissner believes that 'not only had Neanderthal man mastered the art of body painting but he probably believed in a single all-powerful god'.[109]

As well as a sensitivity towards the dead, the Neanderthals cared compassionately for the living, for the weak and the old. The skeleton of an old woman whose body had been crippled from youth with arthritis was found buried ceremonially in a grave, implying a devoted life-long care and respect.

THE CAVE BEAR GOD

A great deal remains to be discovered about the caricatured and often misunderstood Neanderthals. For as well as the burial remains there are other remarkable traces still to be interpreted. In the highest known cave ever to be dwelt in by man, at Drachenloch in Switzerland, two of the chambers contain low stone walls made by the Neanderthals. About three feet high, they run alongside the cave wall leaving a space in between of some fifteen inches. This space is filled to overflowing with the skulls of cave bears which are attached to the first two vertebrae of their spines. Two other neighbouring caves are filled with thousands of bear skulls, many arranged in careful piles.

In one of the Drachenloch chambers there are six rectangular stone chests each covered by a slab of rock which forms a lid. Inside are bones of bears, including the leg bones. One chest holds seven bear skulls placed carefully so that their muzzles point to the cave exit. At the far end of the same chamber three bear skulls have been put together in an empty space between fallen rocks. And yet another skull has been placed with great care beneath a huge stone which was wedged in such a way that it would not fall. This skull was encircled with a crown of stones which followed the shape of the bear's head.

The hip joint sockets had been removed from some of the

skeletons and were used perhaps as the base for oil lamps in the remote darkness of the cave. Some sockets had outer edges highly polished 'as though they had been worn away by generation after generation of human hands'[107]. Were they perhaps sacred vessels used for drinking the blood of the bear? Close beside the cave's entrance a fire-pit had been dug, the ashes still there after at least 70,000 years. Beside the pit was a 'bone altar' on which lay a cave bear's skull which had the bone of another bear piercing its cheek cavity – perhaps part of a ritual sacrifice. This bone altar has been called 'the earliest visible expression of man's regard for an invisible god'.[108] In a nearby cave were thirty small rounded white quartzite pebbles brought from some other region and revealing an early love for white stone which was to continue down the centuries. These too were probably ritualistic – although they might have been used in a prehistoric game! No human bones were found in these caves, which seems to show that they were indeed shrines to the cave bear.

These caves were not the only ones to contain bear skulls. Such ritual burials were found in mountain caves all over Europe, some as high as six thousand feet. One archaeologist has said, 'These skeletal remains could not have got up there or in there by any natural means', so there is no doubt but that such burials were 'a calculated gesture towards an exalted and timeless power'. Offerings are always made to a deity. Ivar Lissnar, who studied the primitive Tungus of Northern Manchuria, found that the practice of offering the skull and marrowbones of the quarry to a supreme god was still taking place: 'The sacrifices of the Siberian peoples . . . are definitely directed toward an invisible being who is the sky and light and universe . . . ' He believes that the prehistoric peoples who sacrificed cave bears also believed in a supreme being and he quotes the prehistorian who investigated the Drachenloch cave as saying, 'This is as archeologically certain as anything of the kind can be'.[109]

Perhaps the great cave bear, infinitely menacing and powerful, might itself have come to represent the God of Death and these skulls were placed in honour and propitiation, for undoubtedly this cave was a holy shrine. Or it might be that the bear had taken on the role of a totem, the 'spirit' of the tribe, and the cave was its holy centre. Or, as Lissnar believes, the 'single all-powerful god' – the ground of all being – had even then been apprehended and the heads of bears, who were perhaps man's greatest adversary and therefore worthy of the strongest respect, had been placed there while still warm with flesh as offerings.

In today's analytical society we regard such customs as clearly belonging to a barbaric and crude form of religion. In showing our repugnance, however, we fail to recognise a spiritual attitude of the greatest importance to early man. For us, the eating of meat is merely a physiological act. But for the Neanderthals both the killing and the eating of prey was almost certainly a sacrament by means of which they communicated with another dimension of spirit. During the many thousands of years of prehistory it appears that all physiological acts, such as eating, were regarded as sacred – they were sacraments by way of which man came near to the reality of Being. Through the ceremonies surrounding such acts, he set himself free from merely automatic responses. By the actions of his daily life, celebrated in ritual and ceremony, he could find and express meaning in a way which freed him from nothingness.

> Man is trying . . . to give 'being' to even his most ordinary and insignificant acts. By its repetition, the act coincides with its archetype and time is abolished. Thus, by transforming all his physiological acts into ceremonies, primitive man strove to 'pass beyond', to thrust himself out of time into eternity. I do not want to stress here the function fulfilled by ritual, but we must note at once that it is the normal tendency of the primitive to transform his physiological acts into rites, thus investing them with spiritual value. When he is eating or making love, he is putting himself on a plane which is not simply that of eating or sexuality.[60]

THE RELIGIOUS MAGIC OF CAVE PAINTING

By 50,000 BCE the Neanderthals had mostly been succeeded by a different race of people who were of average height, well coordinated, strong, muscular and with broad features. Their brain capacity was indistinguishable from ours – indeed, if we could meet the men and women of that time we would not know the difference between them and ourselves.

From evidence in Russia we know that the mammoth was a universal food and that mammoth-hunters lived in tents or huts made of bone frames covered with skin. Mammoth-hunting went on throughout Europe and great piles of mammoth bones have been discovered as far west as England. At Hengistbury Head there is evidence that tents had been erected near the bones, their edges weighted with stones. Archeologists now seriously question whether man might have been the cause of the mammoth's extinction.

But although tents were used for the wandering hunters, caves were still the most popular habitation and it is in this period, particularly between 35,000 and 10,000 BCE, that magnificent and amazing works of cave art were accomplished. There is no doubt but that these paintings were religious. Many caves were available but only a few were used and the work itself was done far inside the inner depths in chambers which must have been considered holy, for generation after generation came to make their mark on these walls and on no others.

Herbert Kühn in his book *The Rock Pictures of Europe*[101] relates how he was taken to an almost inaccessible cavern, first gliding on a small skiff along a subterranean river and then creeping and worming his way through nearly impassable passages. The first hall he reached was full of sculptured rock bisons. Around the sculptures the clay floor had hardened with time to the texture of stone, holding within it the footprints of Ice Age people. Their heel marks had been pressed into the ground, indicating that a circular dance had taken place – perhaps a bison dance to ensure the increase of herds, although another explanation could be that initiation ceremonies took place in this cavern.

In the nearby cave of Les Trois Frères, Kühn tells us, vast halls exist. In the last of them, the most spacious and the most beautiful (and all these caves have a piercing, other-worldly beauty, with their utter silence and strange rock formations which often resemble in colour and shape the inner organs of the body), over five hundred pictures of animals are not only painted but also engraved for all time on to the walls. For such an immensely long period were these caves used as sanctuaries that beneath the uppermost layer of painted bisons on one wall can be seen the great curved tusks of the mammoths, their massive feet and round blue eyes.

At the far end of the sanctuary is the famous 'Sorcerer of Trois Frères', the earliest depiction of a human being. He is poised in a dancing movement with head turned to face the room:

> An eerie thrilling picture, with his large dark eyes he gazes at the visitor. It is impressive, it is even alarming to look steadily into those eyes which for millennia have stared down from a height into vacant space. This shaman wears upon his head the mask of a stag with its antlers. Bear's paws cover his hands and a horse's tail hangs from his waist. One leg is raised in a dance.
>
> No, there cannot be much doubt about it. These prehistoric caves are cult places comparable in their essence with the rock-cut temples of Ellora or Ajanta in India. . . Magic and wizardry had their holy places in the Ice Age, places where beasts were enchanted and by supernatural means brought under the power of man.
>
> In this same cave of Les Trois Frères there are other pictures of shamans or magicians. One of these wears upon his shoulders a bear's fell and is playing a flute. So we may gather that music, of some sort, was used in the ceremonies of the Paleolithic cults. Also in this cavern is the engraving of a naked man disguised in a bison's mask. He is also shown dancing. The bent upper part of the body, the flexed knees, the outstretched arms, the leg held high all remind us of some of the cult dances performed to this day by African, Amerindian and Asiatic tribes.[101]

Such caverns, so dark and difficult to reach, so secret, would have been considered shrines for the protection of the magic of the paintings. It would have been necessary for the shamans to communicate alone with the sacred paintings in the deep dark silence of the cave, to be in touch with the deity who controlled the forces which brought animal and man together. Many Eskimo and Amerindian tribes have a 'lord of the beasts' who is the protector of animals and apportions out the game to hunters as he considers fit.

Was the haunting shaman in Les Trois Frères the earliest portrait of a god that has yet been discovered? The Abbé Breuil came to believe so. He first thought it to be a sorcerer. But between the two guesses of the Abbé Breuil it is extremely difficult to decide – but perhaps not so important to make a choice as modern man might suppose; for if the vivid, unforgettable lord of the animals in the hunter's sanctuary of Trois Frères is a god, then he is certainly a god of sorcerers, and if a sorcerer, he is one who has donned the costume of a god; and, as we know, and see amply illustrated in the ritual lore of modern savages, when the sacred regalia has been assumed the individual has become an epiphany of the divine being itself. He is taboo. He is a conduit of divine power. He does not merely represent the god, he is the god; he is a manifestation of the god, not a representation.

But a picture too is such a manifestation. And so, perhaps, the most likely interpretation is, after all, the second by the Abbé Breuil, namely, that the so-called 'Sorcerer of Trois Frères' is actually a god, the manifestation of a god – who, indeed, may also have been embodied in some of the shamans themselves, during the course of the rites, but here is embodied for us, forever, in this wonderful icon.[35]

Although the outside story of the immense period of time covered in this chapter may seem to consist in the main of bones and stones, the inner story is now beginning to reveal itself in the form of growing imagination and sensitivity, consciousness and spiritual understanding. And it is in the realm of the shaman that we will look for its next expression.

CHAPTER TWO
The shaman and the animal powers

The greatest wonder in the huge caves of France and Spain are the paintings of animals. So splendid are they that their equal has rarely been seen in succeeding cultures. The intensely evoked strength of body – as though the artist was still observing and touching the powerful shoulders, great muscled flanks and heavy head – give the paintings a sense of inwardness, as if the painter was realising the animal within himself. And through his work it is as though we too can apprehend the animal in the same way, inwardly; recognising the sheer animal presence, as if we can feel the power of the hot strong breath and can gaze at the massive neck and brow.

For the paintings reject all non-essentials. The sure, clear lines move sensitively to portray the harmony of limb and trunk. The life and movement of the animal is captured in just a few vivid lines – a high-maned wild horse with neck stretched and legs in flight will suddenly burst upon the eye; a slow, clumsy bear stumbles along; a lion, full-faced, seems to stare at the onlooker. The lines are delicate, fluid and imaginative, reminscent of Chinese Sung drawings. It was this impressionistic vitality which induced the archaeologist Etienne Sourieau to say:

> Everything looks as if (putting it cautiously) the artist has wanted to create a spiritual presence, as close as possible to a real presence, but not a symbolic one. . . . We should not neglect this astonishing and disquieting effect which art as magic must have evoked, independently of all ulterior aims, simply by its power to make the unreal and imaginary into a real and concrete image.[79]

The paintings of the animals are never symbolic. The few representations of humans are often symbolised by stick-like legs or a few indicative lines. Their posture within the caves is often movingly humble, stooping forward as though in awe, their outlines vague and indefinite, although the statuettes and engravings at the cave entrances show an upright position. In contrast, so much living and accurate detail has gone into the animal paintings that it has been possible to distinguish cave bear from brown bear, three breeds of horses, and the staring round-eyed mammoth. It has even been suggested that where a great number of lines appear to be flowing from the same leg joint, that this is an attempt to portray 'cinematic' movement.[107]

What could have been the emotion which so moved the cave artists that their depictions of animals remain unforgettable? It was not the love of art for its own sake. There are many smooth walls near cave entrances which stand unadorned. The greatest paintings are in the darkest and most arduously difficult to reach recesses where men and, for all we know, women, must have been lying on their backs using long rods or crouched sideways, sometimes even lying doubled up. They cut on the rock face by means of stone knives. Almost certainly they used lamps made of grease-soaked moss which could only have cast a feeble and flickering light. Under such impossible conditions some of the world's greatest art was created. Why?

Undoubtedly these paintings were thought of as sacramental. In a foreshadowing of modern man's religion, the cave people seem to have used natural platforms and niches as 'churches', sometimes grand, sometimes small. In these remote sacred places, scenes of the hunt are absent. Instead, the animals gaze down singly, without foreground. That the cave-dwellers knew how to execute group action in the hunt has been established by designs carved on their implements, but for sacred and magical purposes such scenes were not considered appropriate. It was the animal in itself which mattered and not its function as a source of food.

The use of stalagmites and of natural rock formations, such as the stag horns added to a head-shaped depression in the rock at Niaux, seems to show that a feeling of pre-existence, as though the 'being' of the animals was already in the cave, was in the mind of the artist. Within the 'churches' certain areas seem to have had a special mystical significance, for many figures have been imposed one above the other as though each added to the sacredness of the next.

Such evidence points to a mystical empathy with animals which we have lost today. Who exactly were these people who paid such reverence to the source of the food they ate and who lived lives which were centred around a religion which was perhaps as devotional as any we know today?

THE ICE AGE PEOPLE

Modern methods of dating are now able to tell us a good deal about what these people were like. As early as 60,000 BCE a large number of people appeared in Europe, possibly from the Urals and Caspian Sea. They have been called Cro-Magnon from the name of the cave in France where their skeletons were first discovered. There were variations of Cro-Magnon man as there are variations among Europeans today, but they were all recognisably from the same stock. They occupied Europe at the same time as the older race of Neanderthals.

The Cro-Magnons may have developed a form of writing – engravings on wood or bone – but if so this has not yet been deciphered. More likely, though, they felt no need for written communication, for their memory would have been greatly superior to ours. Even now in many eastern countries it is customary to memorise truths rather than to write them down, and it is certainly the way the Vedas and the early Buddhist teachings, as well as many sagas from Norse and Celtic mythology, were carried down the centuries. It is more than likely that Ice Age man. with an instinctual memory of many thousands of years, thought communication other than by speech and deed unnecessary.

The span of time with which we are concerned in this chapter is again an immensity. From 60,000 to 10,000 BCE is approximately the period of Cro-Magnon man. The landscape during his time changed from the wet and cold arctic tundra which followed the fourth Ice Age to a drier although still cold steppe land on which grazed vast herds of bison, wild cattle, horse, antelope, reindeer and mammoth. This is the time of the great hunters.

THE SHAMAN HIMSELF

The famous sorcerer of Trois Frères (described at the end of the last chapter) represented not only a god-figure but also the great magician, the supreme shaman, through whose power the masked dancers moved to the sound of pipes, flutes and drums.

We can begin to assemble a picture of spiritual ceremony from the evidence in the caves; of rituals which led to an extraordinary awareness of the animal life through which these humans saw divinity. Within the blackness and stillness of the vast caves, some of cathedral size, lit only by flickering lamps, the masked figures danced and as they danced felt a sense of transformation, perhaps even of transcendence – a feeling which has echoed down the millennia to human groups in many times and places.

Max Bégouën, in his novel *The Clay Bisons*, recreates the scene for us, one which he has seen among shamanic societies today:

> The Shaman and his neophytes rejoin the initiated who are awaiting them. In the little low room which they have just left, the deep and clear heelprints cross over the ritual signs which the Shaman has carved into the earth. . . . The sacred dance then begins to the beat of the magic drum. With bodies covered in long furry skins and heads hidden in horned masks, the men turn around the altar where the two clay bisons symbolise the fertility of the herd.[14]

The decisive role in all ceremonies was the shaman's. In Trois Frères he dominates the great cave, his round eyes gazing straight at the beholder and carrying immense power. His place in the cave is above all the other paintings and is some twelve feet above the ground – nobody has discovered yet how a painter could have worked at such a height and this adds to the strange, remote magic of the figure itself, as well as the fact that, unlike any of the other figures, it is outlined in black.

Perhaps to emphasise his magic power there are drawings in the same cave of a group of three strangely portrayed figures. One has a man's legs, a horse's tail, a bison's head, and the front two legs of an animal with one hoof cloven. He appears to be dancing and accompanying himself with music on a bowed instrument. In front of him is a female animal, half deer and half bison. The dancing figure seems to be charming her with his music for the great bison head is turned towards him. Leading the little group is a reindeer whose forelegs end in long human fingers. Here is animal magic indeed.

Many archaeologists had adopted the view that this scene

represents hunting magic – that by distorting the creatures the shaman averts their hostility, which would be fierce if their exact resemblances were drawn. But such a theory fails to hold up when we know that so many animals were painted in exact detail elsewhere. It seems more likely that this is an actual transformation scene; and it could only be depicted where it was believed to take place – in the cave where the shaman transformed himself from man into spirit and took his journeys to other worlds.

The shaman is the oldest human manifestation of spirituality known to us, and one which has apparently continued without a break from the Ice Age or earlier up to the present day. He is to be found in many primitive societies, particularly in Northern Siberia among the Gilyaks, in North American Indian tribes, in Eskimos, and among the Aborigines of Australia. It is known that about 20,000 BCE, when shamanism was at its height, there was a wide dispersement of peoples all over the world and it is now believed that where societies and tribes have remained virtually untouched by civilisation the ancient religion has remained much as it was.

The anthropologist Mircea Eliade has shown that shamanism is still the dominant religion of such hunters today; that 'the essential core of shamanism is an "original phenomenon" somehow embedded in the human condition itself, and consequently it is known to all archaic peoples.'[3] He points out that the experience of ecstasy, which the shaman attains, also seems to be an essential element in the human state.

What is a shaman? Much study has been made of shamanism in both primitive and sophisticated societies and it is a great deal easier to answer that question now than it would have been earlier in the century. Shamans are 'specialists of the sacred', men able to 'see' the spirits, to go up into the sky and meet the gods, to descend into the netherworld and fight the demons, sickness and death.[3]

Shamans have discovered the ways of using ecstasy for the good of the community. Through his ecstatic trance the shaman has an 'experience' of the sacred. He is believed to be able to communicate with the gods and with the dead, with animals and birds. By means of his special techniques – which include fasting, meditation and certain drugs – the shaman attempts to transcend the normal state of man. He wants to rise above what is thought of as the unsatisfactory and fallen state and to find once more the primordial consciousness of purity and innocence. Shamanistic societies almost always believe in a lost paradise, a time when heaven and earth were one, when man could talk to the gods and to animals, when the universe had complete access to itself with one shared language for all creatures.

The shaman's ecstasy re-enacts the prefallen state by transcending the time barrier – the existence of time being thought of as a consequence of the 'fall'. But nowadays he reactualises it in the spirit whereas it is believed it used to be in the flesh. To do this, his spirit passes out of his body and travels on mystical journeys through other levels and other worlds. He can retrieve the wandering soul of the person who is ill and bring him back to his body; go with the souls of the dead to their next existence; appeal to the gods for their mercy on the soul of a sacrificed animal.

> . . . the shaman's power rests in his ability to throw himself into a trance at will. Nor is he the victim of his trance; he commands it, as a bird the air in its flight. The magic of his drum carries him away on the wings of its rhythm, the wings of spiritual transport. . . . And it is while he is in this trance of rapture that he performs his miraculous deeds which involve that background . . . reality which for most others is crusted over.[3]

In Ice Age times it must have been communication with animals which mattered most of all. We know from our own day that it is during his initiation period that the shaman encounters an animal who teaches him the language of animals and becomes his companion spirit. This surely reaches straight back to the far-off days when bear, bison, lion, reindeer and mammoth were venerated for their unique spirit and strength. Such veneration among shamanic societies has never been considered a regression to an inferior level. Rather, the animals are thought to be full of immense power and presence in their own right. Thus to be able to speak their language and enter their life is to enhance the human condition by great richness of experience.

The shaman must, before he sets out on his spirit journey, perform the act of 'recovery' of animal friendship – he must restore the prefall accord which animal and man shared. No cosmic journey is possible until he has attained a sense of purity and ecstasy and the ability to act spontaneously (with instant and correct judgment). These qualities are not obtainable in the ordinary world. Consequently he masks and dresses himself as an animal and imitates animal behaviour, as well as giving the cries of animals and birds – this constitutes a dialogue with them in their secret language. While he does this he is accompanied by drumming and a dance of animal-masked dancers.

Ice Age evidence of dancing is plentiful, from feet marks to paintings. Of drumming too there is evidence. For some time it has been believed that a strange type of object found all over Europe is a drum stick. These objects are carved pieces of reindeer horn with a hole worked through at one end. Archaeologists have called them, for lack of a better term, *batons de commandements* (commander's maces). The carving on them is unusually skilled and precise – a design or hunting scene. Shamans among seventeenth-century Lapp reindeer hunters (before modern civilisation had influenced them) used an identical type of baton to beat a magic drum.[79]

Eliade points out that for shamanism today the drum is of the first importance for it enables the shaman to concentrate.[65] The beat of the drum creates a trance state, which is shared by all the group. Then he is able to make contact with the spiritual worlds through which he will travel. By means of the drumming he can fly through the air or summon the animal spirit. The animal that the shaman recalls to life is his other self and when it enters him he changes into this mythical ancestor. During the 'bringing to life' rite, the shaman tells in an appropriate animal voice the whole life-history of the animal up to the moment it was brought down by the hunter. Many present-day tribes talk of a mythical time (perhaps the Ice Age) when each member of the tribe could become an animal and could share in the life of the ancestor. But today it is only the shaman who has that privilege.

THE HEALING SHAMAN

Until quite recently the very word shaman (it comes from Siberia) was relatively unknown. The shaman of Les Trois Frères was usually called a sorcerer or magician, and his magic was thought to be directed solely towards fertility or successful hunting. This reflects a narrowness of understanding, reducing his role to a mere medicine man rather than a mystic.

If we find it hard to believe that the Ice Age hunters had anything but a materialistic desire for food in their mind, we should remember that our present mastery of the natural world has been largely at the expense of the spirit, and our faith has waned as our acquisitiveness has grown. We have lost respect for the things about us and the earth is no longer sacred – a loss which was perhaps foreshadowed in Genesis, when the Hebrew God said, 'And the fear of you and the dread of you shall be upon every beast of the earth, and upon every fowl of the air, and upon all that moves on the earth, and upon all the fishes of the sea; into your hands are they delivered.'[17]

The healing power of the shaman was to bridge the gap between the hunter and his prey; to reconcile the human need for food with the equal need for faith. It was he who kept the two worlds of human and animal in harmony. He did this effectively only because he and all his group must have believed in a god or gods who were exalted and universal. It is very probable that, like the Neanderthals, Cro-Magnon man believed in one universal spirit, the creator of all. Through the shaman they came into communion with this spirit. For the true shamanic experience was the transcendence of the separate self – the self-conscious self – which perhaps first found its expression in the Neanderthals. We cannot know this for certain, but we do know from modern hunters, fishers and herdsman-breeders that because of the transcendence which the shaman attains there is contact with the Source, with the origin of all souls and all worlds.

We should see the shaman then as essentially a healer of the spirit, embodying a quality little understood in the west today. He healed the rift between man's inner and outer worlds. He was the means by which initiates could release themselves from time and dissolve into a chaos from which they could be reborn into the purity of the primal condition. The shaman's ecstasy revealed to his followers another world. It was 'the world in which *everything seems possible*; where the dead return to life and the living die only to live again; where one can disappear and reappear instantaneously; where the "laws of nature" are abolished; and where a certain superhuman "freedom" is exemplified and made dazzlingly *present*.'[62]

THE INDEFINABLE ANTHROPOMORPHS

In two of the French caves there are some strange and rather disturbing figures which seem to differ in kind from other Ice Age drawings. For one thing their sex is impossible to determine. For another, they seem human in a way which is quite unlike the masked dancers of other scenes. Two mobile pieces have breasts beneath animal-like, yet bearded, faces.

They are known as 'anthropomorphs' and have given rise to a number of possible explanations, chief of which is that they represent a wounded or threatened man. There is some evidence for this in the wounded anthropomorphs with darts piercing their animal or bird heads which have been found in the cave of Pech-Merle.

In England there is a similar figure engraved on a bone which was found in the Pin Hole cave of Creswell Crags in Derbyshire. This figure is undoubtedly human yet it has an odd pear-shaped body, belted, with one unshaped stick-like arm and another flipper-like one at the top of the thigh. Its head is enclosed in a horse mask. Although precisely carved, the whole shape gives an extraordinary effect of deliberate vagueness and indeterminism. It is indeed one of the anthropomorphs, but it seems impossible to give it the interpretation of a wounded (there are no signs of wounds) or a threatened man.

British archaeologists have called it the 'masked dancer'. But is it perhaps the shaman himself? It is possible that the anthropomorphs represent the transition the shaman goes through in order to reach ecstasy, when he is neither human nor animal – he is often thought to suffer pain at this period and to feel afraid. Perhaps the anthropomorphs show us the actual moments of change. The Creswell Crags anthropomorph may be reaching, through the sacred dance, the company of animals. Or possibly he is already 'away' on a restorative flight. Transformation and transcendence might both be represented by the very shapelessness of the anthropomorph, and undoubtedly his every feature expressed mysterious power to Ice Age man.

SKELETON POWER

It is the duty of the shaman to restore the oneness of heaven and earth, not only for himself but for his community. By journeying out of time he ends the state of disruption and brings back the lost paradise of animal friendship. He reconnects earth with heaven. In touch with the gods during his flight, he communicates with them and receives their blessing for his tribe.

The Eskimo shaman has a mystical experience as well in which he sees his own skeleton. This experience is of the utmost importance for it means the ability to see both death and resurrection. The shaman's skeleton is the personification of death, but the bones are the means by which he will be reborn to a higher state of existence. Within the Teyjat cave in France, three Ice Age skeletons are dancing, their fleshless ribs a shimmer of movement. In this way the Ice Age is connected to the modern Eskimo (this experience is also known in Central Asia and Tibet).

It brings to the fore the importance which *the bone* had for primitive peoples. By means of interior vision the shaman finds his bones again – which early man probably thought of as the root of all life. With bones there can be rebirth for animals and humans. The flesh disappears but not the bone. The bone seems timeless and was probably thought to be the renewer of the time-bound flesh. To see his bones, the shaman has to move out of time. He reaches the place where he can witness the source of his life.[62]

It is on bone and not painted on a cave that the Creswell Crags shaman is presented. It is easy to ignore the religious art of the British Isles because so little from this period has been discovered. However there is no question of its occupation by Cro-Magnon man (at least in the south) so it must be assumed that a great deal has failed to stand up to the passage of time. In southern England there are no deep caverns sealed off from the air, such as those of Lascaux and Altamira. The rapid decay of the paintings at Lascaux once the cave was opened up shows how ephemeral the art was.

Other engraved bones have been found in Creswell Crags and a whole culture has been called after them – the Creswellian. The caves themselves line the sides of a low gorge and are reflected in a lake at the bottom, which was once a river. The cliffs are of limestone, pitted and cragged, with a covering of brush and pine tree. They are known to have been inhabited some 50,000 years ago by the Neanderthals but a sharp lowering of the temperature, signalling a brief return of the Ice Age glaciers, emptied them for some 13,000 years when they were briefly inhabited again. Yet another empty aeon passed by until around 20,000 BCE they were lived in during the cave-painting era, when the bone engravings were made. Almost certainly there were wall paintings within the caves but they have not survived – although there remain many caves yet to be explored. One thing which has come down to us though is a famous work of art – a horse's head and forebody, beautifully engraved on a fragment of bone and found in the Robin Hood cave.

So fine is it that it easily stands up to the best of the French engravings. The horse as an animal was always admired by cave artists. In the Duruthy cave there is a block of sandstone which has been carved into the bold head and powerful shoulders of a horse. The archaeologist, M. Arambourou, said of it, in words which could apply to the Creswell Crags horse:

> One cannot fail to be struck by the entirely hieratical character of this horse, which owes as much to the posture given to the animal as the manner in which it is executed. With a realism which nevertheless suggests the particular rather than the general, the sculptor has, it would seem, figured not a horse, but the horse. . . .[79]

THE NOTCHES OF TIME

The piece of bone containing the horse's head also has a series of vertical notches superimposed on the horse and continuing along one edge. A number of horizontal lines appear to stream across the horse's body. The superimposing of lines occurs a good deal in the French caves also and has always been a matter of mystery. At first it was thought accidental, due to the blackness of the caves, which must have made the artists almost blind. But this theory does not stand up because of the number of movable objects, such as the Creswell piece of bone, which also contain many lines. Another more likely theory is that the cave walls were sacred and the act of engraving or painting had to be renewed over a long period of time. We can imagine each new initiate having to make a mark. But movable bone needs a different explanation.

In his book *The Roots of Civilisation*,[116] Alexander Marshack has suggested that engraved bones not only show successive additions of one image on another, but actually record intervals of time. Certainly the notches on the Creswellian bone look like a record and not like accidental marks. If Marshack is right, then we must believe that Ice Age hunters were able to observe and record significant events, times and seasons, possibly the movements of the moon. Microscopic study of the lines has shown that flint engraving tools have been renewed many times in the course of one sequence; each part of the marking has been a tiny one, which means that even on one single line a number of marks formed it. Do the different infinitesimal marks add up, then, to some mysterious total?

At the moment nobody knows. But since these engravings have always been connected with the sacred animals, perhaps their significance was also connected with the rituals attendant on the shaman.

THE ANIMAL ANCESTOR

Besides some other pieces of decorated bone, Creswell Crags has not yet revealed any more secrets – except for the possibility of horse worship. An unusual number of horse bones have been recovered there, and as well as the famous horse engraving there is also the shaman's mask which seems to be that of a horse. Instead of the bison of France, it may be that the Creswellians took the horse for their sacred animal; and, if so, the continuity among the English in their love of horses has been remarkable! During this period England was cool and the more exotic animals such as the lion and hyena had left, never to return. The main source of food was horse, reindeer and elk. Whereas in France reindeer was the staple food, it seems that in Britain horses were more common.

Gertrude Levy has pointed out that in shamanic societies of recent date, it has been the custom to take one animal as the embodiment of the ancestral spirit. Its life was maintained through sacrifice by generation after generation. The animal would be reverently sacrificed in order that it would live again. It embodied the soul of each individual in the group; at initiation times he or she would know the experience of unity with all the group through the living force of the totemic animal. An image, such as the Creswellian horse, would represent its magical power.

> The primary group known to us was not that of blood, but of a willed participation in a life both physical and non-physical, which stretched through time to include the dead and the unborn. . . . It appears that in some instances at least, the life-energy of the natural animal was intended to be conveyed to the divine power as well as to his celebrants: that the eating was in fact a sacrament.[107]

Ice Age man's relationship to many of the other species with which he shared the earth was grounded in their common heritage. When he hunted and killed, it was also himself that was killed, and his blood spilt; for the same spirit pervaded all. The animal must die in the hunt but its life would continue in the flesh of those who consumed it. Describing a Red Indian shamanic society, the historian Joseph Campbell says:

> The hunt itself . . . is a rite of sacrifice, sacred, and not a rawly secular affair. And the dance and chant received from the buffalo themselves are no less a part of the technique of the hunt than the buffalo drive and acts of slaughter. . . . The proper sacrifice for the hunter is the animal itself, which through its death and return represents the play of the permanent substance or essence in the shadow-world of accident and chance.[35]

Such beliefs developed over a very long period of time and it is not difficult to imagine that the Ice Age saw the start of them – or perhaps they even went much further back than that. What becomes clear is that the horse in Creswell Crags (as with the bison in Lascaux) was the sacred animal to which the group was spiritually joined; and that the shaman of Creswell Crags invoked the help of the horse on his long journeys to other worlds.

THE CENTRE OF THE WORLD

It is now believed that not only were Ice Age people capable of far greater sophistication in religious understanding than they have hitherto been credited with, but that they also lived by myth. There are certain world myths, such as the myth of the Creator who enters the Primordial Waters either as an anthropomorph or as a water creature and brings back from the bottom of the sea the material to make the world. This myth is so widely disseminated that its origins must go back to earliest prehistory. In the same way, myths about magical flight are documented throughout the world and seem to have an equally ancient origin.[3] They relate directly to the experience of the vast space of the sky with all its wonders of wind and cloud, thunder and lightning, sun and rain. It is here, in endless space, that the gods live with all non-humans, and here that the shaman travels when he communes with them. The planets, stars and moon were also of vital importance, particularly the moon which throughout history was always thought to be especially influential on the life of man. And the stars, slain by the sun, reappear as a symbol of rebirth. A prehistoric night sky was probably fiery with comets and shooting stars. As recently as 729 AD, the Ven. Bede tells us that 'two comets appeared around the sun, striking terror into all who saw them. One comet rose early and preceded the sun, while the other followed the setting sun at evening, seeming to portend awful calamity to east and west alike.'[13]

As well, there would also have been myths connected with darkness. Darkness was holy, for it was only in the very blackest parts of the caves that the shaman's dance took place. It was perhaps the underworld itself from which animal and man first came forth and to which they would return. Descent into the dark earth may have been believed necessary for future rebirth.

Central to shamanic mythology as practised today is the belief in a Centre of the World around which all space and matter revolves. This Centre is thought to be present in a sacred tree, mountain or pillar, which gives the shaman the ascension necessary for his flight. Nowadays it is usually a tree, but Ice Age societies might well have used a rock as a sacred pillar. During the drumming which precedes the climb, the shaman flies (in spirit) around the pillar by virtue of his drum-beat. When he actually ascends, it becomes the cosmic pillar which links heaven with earth and he begins his flight to the Centre of the World. It is he, and through him his community, who has access to the other reality.

We can perhaps look upon the shaman and the power he has over his community in the following way. In ordinary life the physical objects of the world reign over us and possess our imagination and will to an extent that cannot be realised until their power is shaken off, even if only for a brief moment. Our greatest fault, as the Buddha pointed out, is to become so over-involved with the everyday world that the reactions of the mind become automatic and lose their spontaneous life. In the end we feel indifferent to any other form of existence than the superficial level of owning possessions, be they material or living. We prefer to have than to be.

It was as much to shake himself and his people out of this frame of mind as to execute any specific aims that the shaman entered a trance; that his followers performed a dance; that he was drummed into ecstasy. They took part in his shock of awakening to other realities, not because they went into a materially different world, but because they were able to see their own world with new eyes. This has always been the mystical experience, to know the world anew.

THE WINDING LABYRINTH

One of the great mysteries of the French caves has always been the difficulty of access. Why were the sacred places so remote when there were many easier and smoother walls closer to the entrances? It was not to escape from wild beasts because the skulls of cave bears are common in the inner chambers of Gargas and Pech-Merle, and their footprints are embedded with the tracks of human feet on the ledges above the chasms. The tracks of the cave lion too are found within the innermost reaches – in fact, humans were probably much safer at the cave entrances. So why crawl and trudge down cold, dark and narrow passages which sometimes end up in blank walls or in sudden dangerous drops, or at the edge of one of the great black lakes which lie smooth as glass within the caverns? No wind ruffles these stretches of lifeless water and they are uncannily still. Ice Age man must surely have regarded them with dread. The total descent to the sacred chamber can be over half a mile. The two caves of Les Trois Frères and Tuc D'Audoubert, cut off from each other by a fall of rock, have between them at least a mile of labyrinthine climbs and descents.

One explanation might be that nothing is quite so otherworldly, so remote from ordinary life as the absolute blackness and silence of the inner sanctums. Sensory perception is wiped away and only the experience of being remains. Such conditions might have been thought essential to the death and rebirth of the soul.

It is possible too that the idea of the religious procession first took root in these caves. Gertrude Levy and other anthropologists have found many likenesses to Ice Age objects in the ritual vessels of the Australian Aborigines and it is now believed that their origin was in the European Ice Age. Included in their ceremonial customs is the religious procession, which takes a winding path. This winding, the Aborigines say, is a reminder of the efforts of the first ancestor to reach the earth. Might this be a dimly remembered knowledge of our common ancestors who formed a procession into the depths of the earth? The Aborigines visit ten sacred caves during their processional wanderings.[107]

At the entrance to the Gargas caves a design is carved on the rock which archaeologists, for lack of a better term, have called 'macaroni' or 'meanders' since it twists and turns. At Niaux a similar design has the appearance of a plan. Other designs, also resembling charts or plans, have been found in North Africa and eastern Europe. Levy has observed that the Aborigines draw identical designs on the ground. These meanders mean the Ancestral Animal's searching and the place of its arrival on earth. Concentric circles are where he has stopped, and wavy lines mean his time of searching. In the same way, the people themselves dance the pathways between the worlds. They become one with the Ancestor's life as they follow the winding path, and they believe that the way taken by the divine power is itself a current of energy. It seems possible therefore that the labyrinthine path to the remote Ice Age chamber was a divine maze and each chamber might have been conceived as having an increase in power the deeper in it was.[107]

THE SACRED WORLD

In this chapter we have placed ourselves inside the existence of Ice

Age men and women, to discover the values by which they lived. In so doing we have found that in common with relatively untouched societies of today people believed that the world had a meaning in itself; that it was not just inert matter with no purpose except for food-gathering, but that it was radiant with its own significance. In so far as Ice Age humans believed in a creator god, they would have held that the world must itself be implicit with meaning because the god created it. The earth was sacred and all man's acts were part of that same sacrality.

Accordingly, man lived his life on a two-fold level – 'it takes its course as human existence and, at the same time, shares in a trans-human life, that of the cosmos or the gods'.[63] Belief in a god, far more than mastery over fire and stone, was the profoundest way in which man became distinct from animal. In our machine culture it takes a leap of the imagination to envisage a world where all objects had personality and were sanctified because they were created by a divinity. But we need to remember that 'Nothing could be farther from the truth than the facile belief that God only manifests Himself in progress, in the improvement of standards of living, in the spread of medicine and the reform of abuse, in the diffusion of Christianity.'[108]

In putting ourselves inside the skin of our remote ancestors, we have perhaps come into contact with the first, or nearly first, chapter in human mysticism.

CHAPTER THREE
Earth the Mother

Around 10,000 BCE, with the slow retreat of the nothern ice-cap, Europe became warmer and the great herds of bison and reindeer migrated north. With the melting of the ice-cap, Britain gradually became encircled by sea. In the Near East, the nomadic hunting life gave way to settled farming communities, and between 8000 and 5000 BCE Europe too learnt the cultivation of crops. This gigantic change in the social and economic structure of mankind has long been regarded as double-edged. On the one hand, the benefits of a settled life meant the growth of population, cities and civilisations; also the comforting certainty of food dependent on the reliable cycle of the seasons rather than the hazards of the hunt, for man could now *produce* his food. On the other hand, the ownership of land and the pressures of a growing population led to tense situations of possession and greed. The first wars took place around 10,000 BCE – it is firmly held by archaeologists that there were no organised wars in the pre-farming epochs – and the class system probably sprang up about that time too.

We can look upon the former shaman-hunter society as in a sense timeless; the cave, with its changeless stability, was the without-time medium for the life-force of the paintings and the rituals. Eliade believes that the hunters indeed avoided recording time or bringing it into their consciousness because of a 'desperate effort not to lose contact with *being*'.[61] In all likelihood the movement of time was not fully apprehended until the cycle of seed-planting and harvest, of sun and rain, of animal increase with the phases of the moon, had instilled a sense of regularity into human affairs.

It was in this early farming era that the polished stone axe became common. Gertrude Levy sees it as

> the emblem of the gentle life of cleared forest and reaped harvest, as also of the sacrifice of the peaceful beasts who like

> their wild predecessors had a portion in divinity – the axe which was the successor of the painted sign upon the cavern walls of France and Spain and a forerunner of the Cross – bound the Neolithic region with the progressive civilisations of the Bronze Age.[107]

She believes it also bound together the two aspects of religion as they were developed in east and west – the one connected with the fertility rites attendant on animals and people, the other more involved with stone and the building of altar and tomb in the great Age of Stone which followed.

Mother Earth became the one deity for both aspects of religion and her symbol was the polished axe. As men and women began to feel the pull of opposing forces not only in climate but also in personal attachment to land or village, the Mother kept an ancient role as the earth from which all is born and to which all returns. There is no record in western Europe until the end of the Stone Age of any male god, but there are many records of the Mother-Goddess who was the object of devotion and whose abode was the earth.

RELATIONSHIP WITH THE EARTH

When the Pope alights in a new country his first gesture is to kneel down and kiss the ground. This is a sign of his intense respect and devotion to that part of the earth – a feeling which most of us have at some time or other, particularly about our own land. Exiles long to be buried in their native soil and many people have a deep feeling of belonging to a place even more than to their family.

The Pope re-enacts what may be a very ancient religious rite, for the mystical bonding of mankind to earth found its expression in the Divine Mother who was herself the earth. Children arose from her, to be born by women who were merely the means of their emergence; the real creator was the Earth herself and mothers the method of her completion. Certain places were believed to be especially holy – a cave or spring, tree or rock – and it was here that a woman became pregnant, the new soul entering her from the earth itself.

And at death came the comfort of returning to the Great

Mother, the cycle completed, renewal in her hands a certainty. The body could be laid to rest in the 'mother-land'.

The marvel of the female and her links with the moon and earth could be witnessed in a way which is next to impossible today. For now we know everything with our minds and little remains of wonder to us. But the mystery of woman was as awesome as birth and death. Her menstrual cycle came in accord with the movements of the moon. The child emerged from her body and the milk flowed. Our intellects have objectified and reduced the whole of existence to concepts and we have forgotten that

> the creative magic of the female body is a thing of wonder in itself. And so it is that, whereas the men in their rites (as initiates, tribal dignitaries, shamans, or what not) are invariably invested with magical costumes, the most potent magic of the womanly body inheres in itself. In all her primary epiphanies, therefore, whether in the paleolithic [old Stone Age] figurines or in the neolithic [new Stone Age], she is typically the naked goddess, with an inconographic accent on the symbolism of her own magic form.[35]

The mystery of birth, in which woman acts as the guardian of entry from another world, was apprehended with awe and reverence. The early farming world became filled with the image of the Mother, from the little statuettes of Eastern Europe, Greece and Mycenae to the great earthworks built in her honour, the largest of which is in Britain.

IMAGES OF THE MOTHER

Such statuettes give us our first sight of the Mother. They were first created even before the cave paintings and long before farming had begun. When Cro-Magnon man migrated into Europe in 60,000 BCE, he seemed to discover a love of rock-carving. He was already familiar with the art of stonework through his flint tools, but now he included many images. His sculptures were often of animals but by far his most exciting works of art were small statuettes of women, now agreed to be the earliest portrayal of the human figure ever found. They have been discovered all over Europe from France to Russia, although not in

Spain. Scholars have given the name of 'Venus' to the statuettes after the first one found in Willendorf in Austria which was very curvaceous. Most are between five and twenty-five centimetres in height, carved out of mammoth tusk, bone, limestone or other rocks, and wonderfully stylised to give emphasis to great buttocks and heavy breasts – the effect strangely modern.

The very mother-heaviness of these statuettes can arouse in women a strong feeling of identification – far greater than with a male god. The former nun Meinrad Craighead says:

> I came upon a photograph in a textbook and I recognised my Mothergod. It was a picture of the Venus of Willendorf. The recognition was immediate and certain. I knew this was she whom I had heard in the water and whose face I sought beyond the water. . . . This discovery brought a sense of relief and well-being and gratitude that has never diminished.
>
> But she had no face. The Venus was crowned with waves of water, covering the head, overshadowing the face. It was her entire body that spoke, her breast-belly body, a thick bulb rooted, pushing up a halo of water, water that moved within me. Thereafter it was she whom I sought to see always, and being with her was undoubtedly the origin of my desire for a life of contemplative prayer and to be an artist. I had then, and still have, but one essential prayer: 'Show me your face.'[47]

Meinrad Craighead expresses the extraordinary power which ancient objects can exert on the feelings. Whether a statuette or a flint tool, fitting smoothly into the hand, there is movingly strong body-sense of relationship with earth and rock.

When the Willendorf Venus was found it was thought that such figures were intended to be erotic – hence Venus as their name – and the idea of a fertility cult, which had long been thought likely, was established. But since that first discovery much effort and research has brought to light some hundred and thirty of these female images, all from early Cro-Magnon times, and it now appears that the conclusion about the fertility cult was wrong. Slim figures, without emphasis on breast or hip, are in fact more common than the massive ones. So another explanation is needed.

One possibility might lie in the fact that most of the figurines (which are never masked and often have graceful heads – one

French one even wearing a cap or coif of hair) lack feet, and this was because they were stuck into the ground at the site of a hut or cave mouth. Several have been found placed in shrines and so it is now certain that they were religious objects. This seems to point to an intense feeling for the female body as being itself the divine focus of spiritual forces, and possibly to a religion which was dedicated to this mystery.

Small larch and aspen female figurines are carved to this day by the Siberian reindeer hunters. They are left to guard the hut when the hunt is on, and when it is over they are 'fed' by the hunters with groats and fat. An authority on this society says, 'The psychological background of the idea derives from the feeling and recognition of woman, especially during her period of pregnancy, as the centre and source of an effective magical force.' He also observes, 'The . . . Venus figurines come to us as the earliest detectable expression of that underlying ritual idea which sees in Woman the embodiment of the beginning and continuance of life as well as the symbol of the immortality of that earthly matter which is in itself without form, yet clothes all forms.'[35]

During the later era of the shaman, the making of the little statuettes appears to have stopped in France although some have been found in other countries, including the possibility of one in Grimes Graves in England. Grimes Graves are prehistoric flint mines, deep trenches within a great area of hummocky ground, and the little figurine discovered there is a very rounded Venus carved in chalk. In front of her is an altar composed of blocks of flint in the form of a triangle (the female symbol), with seven deer antler picks resting on it. Although the mines themselves are later than the Cro-Magnon era, yet certain pits are thought to have been started in Cro-Magnon times – the whole area contains three hundred and sixty shafts and must have supplied most of Europe with flint tools. The figurine itself corresponds more to the Willendorf Venus than to later works.

The animal-shaman cave paintings seem to have supplanted these early female figurines, perhaps making 'a shift from the vagina to the phallus in their magic, and therewith, perhaps too, from an essentially plant-oriented to a purely animal-oriented mythology'.[35] It is probable that from 60,000 to 30,000 BCE was a time when the groups were not nomadic but comparatively stationary. Climatically it was a good time for plant-gathering and, as well, the mammoth was plentiful and easily trapped. Within the protection of tent or cave the influence of women might have been better experienced and appreciated than when life again became wandering.

However women do appear in the cave paintings and there are certain indications that some may have also been shamans. Although no statuettes were made then, there is evidence that women were still highly thought of. In the sanctuary of Laussel in southern France, a woman with large hips and breasts is carved on the wall near the entrance. She is holding a bison's horn in her right hand – a symbol for woman which was to become widespread over Europe – and her arm is raised up to shoulder level. Two other women carved from stone but now broken lie near her, also holding horns in their right hands. In later forms of religious belief, and perhaps at that time too, the creative force of the animal was thought to be ejaculated through the horn tip and it has been suggested that these women with horns were helping the hunt by releasing the magic force. It seems here that although the mammoth had by that time been replaced by the bison, the simple magic of the Mother had not yet given way to the more complicated rites of the masked shaman. Indeed such magic may have contributed to the whole shamanistic understanding. From these carvings we can deduce that Cro-Magnon women took part in the magical hunting rites.

This view is supported by other strange carvings. In the cave of La Madeleine a stone was found which was carved on one side with the figure of a shaman, his human features visible beneath the animal mask, while on the other side is a female figure whose animal head may not have been intended as a mask. Was she also a shaman? And was she already transformed into the animal deity? There may be another, even more religious, explanation. Among the cave paintings are some hermaphrodite figures, a strange blend of male and female. Could it be possible that, at least for some engravers, true divinity was recognised as embracing both sexes? If so, this apprehension was more profound than many of our religious ideas today.

In the little 'chapel' of Les Combarelles there is an engraving of a ritual dance in which a stooping man and woman are both clothed in skins and wear tails. Their heads are obliterated by stalactites but were certainly masked. In this same cave other women in animal masks mingle with men. And a few of the Venus statuettes show what has been called an 'apron' trailing from their buttocks, which has now been recognised as representing fur or a tail for an animal dance.

So we can be sure that women not only took part in the ceremonies but probably were themselves shamans – as indeed a number of them are today among the Siberian tribes. The power of woman was still strong, even within the hunting group.

In his book *Up From Eden*, Ken Wilber explores the idea that worship of the female had two aspects. One was the 'Great Mother', and perhaps the Cro-Magnons with their little enshrined figures (always found in places of occupation, but not deep within the caves) saw woman in this way:

> The Great Mother, then, is initially representative of global, bodily, separate and vulnerable existence in space and time. . . . Just as in the infant, the great mother is the one partner with whom the baby plays out the separation drama, so also the infant mankind in playing out its early drama of separation from nature ('mother nature') and from fusion with the environment (the Great Surround), had as its constant partner the Great Mother. The Great Mother came thus to represent bodily existence itself, matter and nature, water and earth, and life and death in that naturic realm.[171]

Wilber compares the Great Mother with the Great Goddess who represented the 'initial insights into a truly transcendental Oneness, a Oneness that is not simply the naturic background of the Great Mother or Earth Mother, but rather the one Form and Divine Ground of all space and time'.[171]

It is the Great Goddess whom we will encounter many times down the millennia. But before leaving the enchanted world of the shrine, the shaman and the cave and advancing forward some several thousand years to that era of settled farming with which we began this chapter, we should take a look at the symbols which were first developed during the Cro-Magnon epoch – symbols which seem to have accompanied the worship of the female as Mother-Goddess for as long as she has existed.

THE LANGUAGE OF SYMBOLS

It is now known that although in western Europe the making of the female statuettes seemed to stop during the cave-painting period, in eastern Europe the worship of the Mother not only continued but if anything increased. In particular the area between the Dnieper and the Don has shown a rich deposit of the Venus figures. The art, however, was not the vivid impressionism of the cave paintings but rather was stylised in a geometric way. The figure of the masked shaman is absent but instead there is 'the perfectly naked fertile female, standing as guardian of the hearth'. All around her are engraved 'a constellation of motifs' and symbols, such as triangles and lozenges, which were to continue in time both in the east and the west.

They were 'the meander (as a reference to the labyrinth), the bird (in the dovecotes of the temples of Aphrodite), the fish (in the fish ponds of the same temples), the sitting animals and the phallus'.[35]

In the region of the Dnieper a number of mammoth skulls arranged in a circle were found. At the centre of the circle was a Venus statuette – to be called by Joseph Campbell 'our Lady of Mammoths'. On this same site, six fine birds carved from mammoth ivory were also discovered, their underwings engraved with swastikas – the earliest swastika yet to be found. Campbell believes it might refer to the labyrinth, but since this site was not connected with the French labyrinthine recesses it is perhaps more likely that the swastika represented a bird in flight.

The flying bird motif (later to be associated with the Bird Goddess) occurred again in the most famous of the early Cro-Magnon burials. The skeleton of a small child was discovered buried at Malta in the Lake Baikal region of Siberia, an area where shamanism still exists today. It is also a region from which some of the North American Indian tribes derived. Campbell sees it as the centre of an 'archaic cultural continuum' going on to the rock shelters of France, farther forward to the Blackfoot buffalo dance of the nineteenth century, and still onwards to the shamanism of the present Siberians, Lapps and Finns.[35]

Within the burial site were found twenty female statuettes of mammoth ivory, all naked except for one which was dressed in the engraved skin of a cave lion – perhaps a shaman's robe. Among the many beads, pendants and medallions which had decorated the body of the child, one showed an engraving of three cobra-like snakes, while another had a design of a spiral with seven turns enclosed in three spiralled S-shapes. An ivory fish had a spiral labyrinth stippled on its side; there were six flying birds in the grave and another on a necklace round the child's neck; also an ivory baton of the sort used in shamanic rites.

This wealth of symbolism seems to indicate an Ice Age sphere of magic. The serpent, labyrinth and bird probably represented the shaman's flight, the spiral was a symbol of water and lunar fertility, and the twenty goddesses were the protectors and ensurers of a new birth. Thus a rich language was revealed by these symbols and much of it was to continue almost up to the present day. Particularly in eastern Europe, where worship of the Mother lasted longer than in the west, such symbols were to remain intact for thousands of years, eventually becoming the basis for much of the symbol language of western Europe as well. Marija Gimbutas has pointed out in her book *The Goddesses and Gods of Old Europe* that the bird in particular became identified with the Mother. Portrayals of birds were common among the cave paintings also and were sometimes drawn as bird-woman hybrids.[70]

Statuettes of water birds such as crane, goose, heron and duck were sacred to the northerners, who must have regarded them as both food and the divine source of food. They are frequently covered with engraved geometric signs such as chevrons, which represented flying, and the meander which was the water over which they flew. The long neck of the bird was often linked with the phallus:

> a phallic Bird Goddess dominates during the seventh and sixth millennia in the Aegean area and the Balkans. Sometimes she is a lifelike erect phallus with small wings and a posterior of a woman, which, if seen in profile, is readily identifiable as a bird's body and tail. Or she may take the form of a nude female figurine with a disproportionately long and massive neck which obviously represents a phallus, as in a marble figure from Attiça. 'Bisexualism' is reflected in bird-shaped vases with cylindrical necks. . . . The concept of the fusion of the sexes occasionally reappears in representations

> of hermaphroditic figures . . . [perhaps a continuation of the hermaphrodites of the French cave paintings] having male genital organs and female breasts. Such figures have beaked heads and sharply protruding posteriors.[70]

The Goddess also came to be closely associated with the snake, the vehicle of immortality because of its ability to shed its skin and be born anew each year. The Snake Goddess usually has stripes or snakes spiralling around her, snakes entwining her, or snakes for her legs and arms. She can appear as both Bird and Snake Goddess in one single divinity. 'She is one and she is two, sometimes snake, sometimes bird. She is the Goddess of water and air, assuming the shape of a snake, a crane, a goose, a duck, a diving bird. The combination of a water snake and a water bird is a peculiarity of the Old European symbolism representing divine ambivalence.'[70]

The snake is symbolised in an abbreviated way by zigzag lines, dotted bands or spirals, the bird of vees, chevrons and crossed chest bands. The snake, as Goddess of Waters, was celebrated by a wealth of water themes which are often abbreviated to labyrinthine meanders. As a begetter of rain she is shown as a naked woman, sometimes with an animal mask, holding out a basin. Her great eyes and triangular beak, or snake, imply that she was a Life Goddess, the source of the cosmos.

Worship of her was abundant in Minoan Crete and Greece. Minoan art in particular is steeped in snakes and birds, with women gracefully wound about with snakes or wings. Terracotta birds were placed in shrines, very often in threes, and the number three seems to have been sacred to the Cretans and Greeks, as it also came to be in other societies. Jugs were shaped like water birds and decorated with symbols of flowing water, which were groups of vertical lines and bands of dots.

Such a language was to remain in use for many centuries after the birth of writing.

THE MOON AS MOTHER

Death and resurrection are the great themes which dominate all religions. From early onwards the Mother became linked with the moon, which was the very symbol of both the end of life and a new beginning – there is always a new moon. The sky is dark for three nights but on the fourth night the moon is reborn. In the same way the dead were also thought to find a new life. Thus death itself was not, with rebirth a certainty, an extinction but was a change, another kind of 'existence'. Death belonged to a different 'life'.[63] As the agricultural peoples discovered the cycle of plants they came to see the earth as related to the moon, and believed that the dead either went to the moon or the underworld in Mother Earth to be given the necessary powers of regeneration.

The moon itself was not their actual object of worship. A natural object in itself was not what was adored, but rather its sacredness lay in what it revealed of ultimate Reality. By the very quality of its being it was an incarnation of that transcendent reality which man has always felt part of and known to be manifest in the world.

The moon was the theophany which revealed the infinite Reality; and all the goddesses and gods, the symbols and myths which became connected with it throughout history have acknowledged its sacred power. It became seen as the Great Mother's manifestation for it governed the waters (tides and rains) and it was the water which quickened the vegetation. In India it was thought that rain came from the moon, and rainfall as such has always been connected with the phases of the moon. When disaster struck, such as a deluge or flood, it was not considered to be a final cataclysm for the moon would bring back the new vegetation and the new humanity. The role of the moon was both to be and to become. It underwent death and yet remained immortal, and its death was never an end but a pause for regeneration. In all moon rites, symbols and myths, man has allied himself to this destiny.

Thus the Great Mother and the moon were interconnected through the fertility of people, animals and crops; and inexhaustible life emerged from the Mother by way of the moon. The main symbol which came to characterise the goddesses of fertility through the succeeding thousands of years was the horns of the ox, or the bull, which represented the moon. Whenever they are found they are the emblems of the divine and fertile Mother. In the language of symbols, the double-headed axe came in time to represent the horns. One horn is the image of the new moon and two is the full moon. 'Clearly the ox's horn became a symbol of the moon because it brings to mind a crescent; therefore both horns together represent two crescents, or the complete career of the moon.'[63] The carved women in the cave of Laussel with their horns in their right hands show us how ancient this emblem is.

Certain animals became symbols of the moon too because something about them, either shape or behaviour, resembled the characteristics of the moon:

> the snail which goes in and out of its shell; the bear which disappears in midwinter and reappears in the spring; the frog because it swells up, submerges itself, and later returns to the surface of the water; the dog, because it can be seen in the moon . . . the snake because it appears and disappears, and because it has as many coils as the moon has days. . . .[63]

Very often each of the symbols, especially the snake, has in the course of time taken off and produced a whole variety of other meanings and associations. So that in the end we are left with a mesh of beliefs, sometimes verging on superstitions (how many people turn the money in their pockets at the new moon?) which have attached themselves to new gods and other situations. It is not possible to mention them all here but we can appreciate that the light of the moon and its descent into darkness is the starting point; and that the Great Mother shares in the immortal nature of the moon as much as she does in the earth.

Professor Eliade gives us a brief look at the groupings which he calls 'lunar metaphysics'. These are the ways in which certain aspects of moon and Mother appear together. Fertility, which means woman, water and vegetation, as well as the 'mythological ancestor' [which could be the totem animal ancestor]; regeneration, which connects us with the serpent and the lunar animals, the 'death and resurrection' of initiates; time, linked with destiny, in which the moon 'measures' or 'weaves' destinies and brings together different cosmic levels; change, which is marked by the opposition of light and darkness or 'by the balance between being and non-being, the virtual and the actual (the symbolism of hidden things; dusky night, darkness, death, seeds and larvae)'.[63]

From the first Venus statuettes of 60,000 years ago to the agricultural peoples of 2000 BCE the myths and religious rites of the Earth Mother were always to do with the mystery of life itself, the actual *appearance* of life being the greatest mystery of the universe; for, to early man, every object from stones and plants to birds and people had a sacred value, a meaning as a sign of the Great Reality. In this way the Mother represented not only the fecundity of life but also its mystery. We still pay unthinking honour to her today when we use the term 'Mother Nature'.

FROM MOTHER TO GODDESS

If we were to sum up the early religious experience of mankind we could say that of the first importance to him was the earth itself. Its solidity and immense variety created an experience of cosmic wonder. Its sacred nature was never in doubt and it manifested a multitude of equally sacred forms – rocks, trees, water, shadows, animals. It was the basis of all existence and all that was on earth was thus interrelated, inseparable, making up one totality. Each form, however insignificant, revealed the reality of the whole, hence the reverence and the guilt for that which had to be taken for food. And hence too the feeling that the Earth was a great womb which gave birth to the whole of creation. The Earth, then, was the earliest spiritual experience of mankind.

It presented itself as Mother because of its ever-fruitfulness and fertility. All living forms came out of its substance and both life and death were seen as part of its eternal cycle, there being a pre-existence and a post-existence. Woman was the link with earth and with moon through the events of her body.

With the course of time and the growth of settled agricultural communities, the Earth Mother gave way in popular belief to the Great Goddesses, a multitude of fertility and hunting divinities with whom we will be concerned in later chapters. They no longer represented the cosmos, as did the Earth Mother. Their roles were less mighty and more confined, but clearer and more dramatic. 'The turning of the Earth Mother into the Great Goddess of agriculture is the turning of simple existence into living drama.'[171]

For when hunting was absorbed by farming a whole revolution in values and sense of time began. Undoubtedly it was a slow-growing and undramatic changeover, but by the time agriculture had become the main means of livelihood man's relationship with the animals – that strange and mystical symbiosis of the Ice Age –

had come to be replaced by what Eliade calls 'the mystical solidarity between man and vegetation'.

> If the bone and blood until then represented the essence and sacrality of life, from then on it is the sperm and the blood that incarnate them. In addition, women and feminine sacrality are raised to the first rank. . . . The fertility of the earth is bound up with feminine fecundity; hence women become responsible for the abundance of harvests, for they know the 'mystery' of creation. It is a religious mystery, for it governs the origin of life, the food supply and death. The soil is assimilated to woman. Later, after the discovery of the plough, agricultural work is assimilated to the sexual act.[58]

The 'mystery of creation' is a mystery which

> demands the 'death' of the seed in order to ensure it a new birth, a birth all the more marvellous because accompanied by an astonishing multiplication. The assimilation of human existence to vegetable life finds expression in images and metaphors drawn from the drama of vegetation. . . . This imagery nourished poetry and philosophical reflection for millennia, and it still remains 'true' for contemporary man.[58]

Neither agriculture as such nor the seed in itself were the subjects of spiritual devotion but rather they represented the vast enigmas of death and rebirth; and such cosmic apprehensions found their expression in the great earthworks of the next age, built to portray the rhythm of fecundity which, like the vegetation it was identified with, revealed the central mystery – the yearly revival of the world. For fecundity became elevated to a spiritual dimension and its ritual activities all revolved around this great enigma, called by Eliade 'the periodical renewal of the world'.[63]

Accompanying the Great Goddess into this age came many of the symbols we know – the bird (often a dove), the serpent, the polished stone double-axe representing her fertility and also herself, and the ox-horns of the fertile moon-earth-Mother. Sacred pillars and trees also came with her, while wild beasts followed her and horned animals were sacrificed to her. It is under a multitude of new names and roles that we will meet her again down the centuries. She has been the longest continuous spiritual idea in mankind's history and was also the strongest until the male god of the Hebrews and Christians, and that of the Norsemen, supplanted her in more recent times.

CHAPTER FOUR
Sun, moon and earth temples

Until quite recently – even as late as 1977 – it was thought that the ancestors of western European farmers came from the Middle East. They were supposed to have journeyed round the Mediterranean to the coasts of Spain and Portugal and then followed the Rhone into northern France. Some time between 5000 and 4000 BCE they were believed to have crossed the Channel into Britain and Ireland.

Some may indeed have followed this route, but recent evidence from carbon dating in Ireland shows a totally different time scale and therefore probably a different history altogether. As early as 7,500 BCE Ireland was populated by communities who had plenty of material equipment and were living as hunters, gatherers and early farmers. Whether they were the indigenous occupiers of the land or came from Britain or directly from Brittany is open to doubt. But what can no longer be doubted is that the Irish people very early on developed a unique and sophisticated understanding of the movements of the sun and moon which was certainly religious in purpose and ahead of others in the world. The first megalithic (huge-stoned) burial passage was at Carrowmore and is dated 4,200 BCE, while the great Boyne complex of Newgrange followed on a thousand years after that simple and powerful beginning.

The communities of the temperate north and west of Europe have left to us what seem to be indelible religious marks – the great earthworks of causewayed camps, long barrows, henges, the strange cursus and the stone-lined passage graves which sprinkle Britain, France, Germany, Holland, Belgium and Scandinavia.

The immensity of effort and labour which was put into those massive mounds (Durrington Walls took a million man hours to construct, the work of years for hundreds of people doing nothing else) has always baffled the older archaeologists who were not always ready to believe that there might be a religious purpose behind the labour. Fortunately it is considered proper nowadays to accept the religious dimension of the Stone Age and younger archaeologists look at it with a more sympathetic and imaginative eye. This has resulted in a great leap forward in knowledge.

At the time of the first megalithic buildings, agriculture was still young and much of western Europe was a wilderness of forest within which the early farmers axed clearings for their settlements and villages rather as the first Canadian immigrants did. The trees were birch, oak, pine, elm and lime, edged by hazel thickets. There was marshland in abundance. River travel or pathways through the forest connected one village with another and the sense of the dark green silent depths of the woods must have been always present. Bears, wolves, lynxes and boars would have caused some danger to travellers. Even now it is possible in the remoter regions of the Massif Central in France to feel a sense of primitive wariness in the wild and lonely country. But the same forest which could awe and terrify was also the provider of housing, warmth and an inexhaustible supply of food. The treacherous marshland contained eels in abundance as well as water-fowl. Materially the forest-dwellers lived well and when agriculture increased even better, although in simple fashion. Spiritually they almost certainly surpassed us in communal worship and devotion.

TEMPLES OF THE SUN

Ireland, with its blue mountains and soft skies, its white drifting bog cotton and lonely pools, was greener and milder than today. The present moors and bogs were probably formed, at least in part, by prehistoric tree clearance, and trees still covered much of the land. Where the River Boyne takes a turn before it empties into the sea, three strange and magnificent structures, known as megalithic mounds or passage graves, dominate the beautiful valley. These are the mounds of Newgrange, Knowth and Dowth and below them lies a multitude of smaller mounds and standing stones. Newgrange is surrounded by the remains of a stone circle, the diameter of which is exactly the same as the smaller circles at Avebury.

The name 'passage grave' means exactly that – a grave at the end of a passage. At Newgrange a wonderfully decorated stone which was once used to seal the entrance has been pushed aside. From this entrance a passage sixty-two feet long has been revealed. It leads to the centre of the mound. Upright stones form walls which support great roof slabs, rising in height as they approach the chamber at the far end. This fine chamber has a perfectly corbelled roof which soars to twenty feet above the floor and is sealed by a single capstone. Three small burial rooms open off the chamber. Above the stone roof, earth has been heaped to form a mound or small hill.

Two circumstances single out these mounds as being the work of a sophisticated and spiritually inspired people. The first is that Newgrange has been found to be aligned to the position of the rising sun on the shortest day of the year. The other is that the three mounds between them contain one of the largest accumulations of late Stone Age art in the western world, most of it symbolic and abstract. These two factors relate to one another.

The art historian Martin Brennan describes in his book *The Stars and the Stones*[26] how he studied the Boyne mounds and the lesser known but even older mounds in the Loughcrew Mountains some forty miles away, feeling that the religious art of the megaliths had been ignored by archaeologists. In March 1980 he and a friend waited patiently at Loughcrew for rainy mountain weather to clear up. He had formed the impression that these older mounds would have been used to record the position of the sun and moon at equinox and 'cross-quarter' days, which are vital for the agricultural calendar. In 1980, the spring equinox (the date when night and day are of equal length) was due on 20th March. But it looked only too possible that cloud would blot out the vision he hoped for at Cairn T, the highest and most central of the passage graves. But at pre-dawn on 17th March, near enough to the equinox for the effect to be identical, the sky was brilliantly clear and the two men set out.

> We were winding up the mountain road when the disc of the sun broke on the horizon. We felt as if we were ten minutes late for an appointment made over 5000 years ago. From the top of the road there would be a climb on foot to the mound perched on the summit of the mountain. The lock on the modern door leading to the passage had frozen during the

night, and as we struggled with it the rising sun was already above the horizon. When we drew back the door a narrow chink of light streamed down the passage and flashed into the end recess of the chamber.

On the upper left of the backstone a rectangular patch of light was rapidly beginning to take form, brilliantly illuminating the entire chamber in a glowing splendour of shimmering golden orange light. It was dazzling, and when we entered the chamber we stood back and gazed in awe. Naturally, we had expected to see something similar to what we had seen at Newgrange. There, the low angle of the sun rising at winter solstice causes the beam of light to sweep across the chamber. Here, however, the light assumed a clearly defined geometric shape that was projected on to the upright backstone and moved diagonally across it, tracing the path of the sun against a mural of prehistoric art. What impressed us most was the careful and delicate modelling of the light beam by the huge stones forming the passage and chamber, and how the shape of the beam conformed to the patterns engraved on the stone. For the first time we were seeing the signs and symbols in the context in which the artist had meant them to be seen. Suddenly markings that had appeared to be random and haphazard became part of an intricately structured system that derived its meaning from the solar event we were witnessing.[26]

His book also captures the fascination with which these two twentieth-century men saw the winter solstice at Newgrange, the most famous of the megaliths. For in Newgrange, a window box built by the original builders into the roof above the entrance allows the sun to strike the end wall on the shortest day of the year. It illuminates a quantity of spirals, eye shapes and lozenges carved into the walls, including rayed discs of the sun, which cannot be seen easily at any other time.

Brennan points out that the passage and chamber of such a megalithic mound as Newgrange is a precise, complex and specialised instrument. Whereas in even earlier times the shadow from a positioned vertical object such as a standing stone or post would have sufficed to show either the time of day or the season of the year, the megalithic mounds brought such calculations to a fine art by narrowing a beam of light instead of merely casting a shadow. Such 'light-beam dialling' does not need an observer to watch the sun's shadow at sunrise because it clearly defines both the height and the direction of the sun after it has risen.

The construct of Newgrange appears to be older than any other in the British Isles, although even older ones exist in northern France. This fact has been a shock to many archaeologists. Before radio carbon dating it was believed that the art of positioning the sun had come from Egypt and the Middle East and that backward Europe was the final repository of a brilliant but foreign technology. When it became apparent that both the Newgrange complex and the passage graves of Brittany were built before the Pyramids and even before the Great Temple of Armun at Karnak, where a similar light-beam technique was used for observing the sun, there was consternation, and since then a continuing deep silence from the older archaeologists. Sceptics point out that the tilt in the earth's axle has changed slightly over the last 5000 years, which would affect the rising position of the sun in relation to Newgrange. But in reality, the shift is only half a degree to the north of the original position and the accuracy of the alignment is hardly affected.

THE MOON CALENDAR

Filled with the excitement of discovery, Brennan and his friend then found that, just as Cairn T caught the sunrise at the equinoxes and Newgrange did at the winter solstices, so did Cairn T – and probably others as well – also capture the full moon.

> The first thing we noticed was that observing moonbeams is quite different from observing sunbeams. Before the sun rises the sky begins to brighten in the east and diffused light enters the chamber. On the night of April 1 we sat in total darkness. We were surprised by the sudden appearance of a mysterious thin shaft of silvery white light which penetrated the passage and created a glowing patch of brightness on one of the chamber stones. We watched in amazement as the size of the patch of light diminished rapidly until it disappeared before our eyes. It was like an apparition, and we were grateful that

> David O'Hehie was present to photograph it, as it was singularly the strangest and yet most beautiful event we had witnessed inside a passage mound. After that I never doubted that, whatever the achievements of the megalith builders in the field of astronomy, the structures they built had a strong element of ritual observation in their function.[26]

They then had to determine whether the lunar orientations were as deliberate as those for the sun. Could they be a random accident? They came to believe that over a long period of time observation of the moonbeams would give a repetition of patterns to form a reliable 18.6 monthly calendar – the time it takes the moon to travel through all its positions. A similar passage mound in Brittany – Gavrinis – is aligned to the moon rather than the sun. But the strongest evidence of moon alignments came from the rock engravings within the mounds, which celebrated the moon in wonderful designs.

Brennan went on to discover that the entrance stones at both Newgrange and Knowth have vertical carved lines on which a shadow falls from a standing stone outside the entrance – at Newgrange on the winter solstice and at Knowth on the equinox – thus giving an external as well as an internal knowledge of time. He also discovered that Dowth was aligned to the *setting* sun at the winter solstice. He has established beyond doubt that the Irish passage graves were superb astronomical observatories and that the west rather than the east was the origin of such wisdom.

WORSHIP AND RITUAL

Yet however useful such observations were for the planting and gathering of crops, it is quite impossible to imagine that this was their sole function. Ninian Smart points out that religion – and these temples were above all religious – is not just a means to an end:

> Religion, and man's relationship to deities, are not simply means to certain ends. They are not simply instruments whereby men promote the solidarity of the tribe and the security and fertility of the food supply. It is true that these last concerns are quite obviously of the greatest importance

> to people struggling in a difficult environment, and it would be surprising if these concerns did not appear in a fairly central way in religious rituals and beliefs. But also men have seen the world as transfused with significances of a different order.
>
> For the primitive, as indeed for many folk who have a strong religious sense, the world is not just a beautiful or ugly place, a difficult or easy habitat, a place for living in: they have also seen it as an awe-inspiring, sacred, holy environment, in which the forces of the unseen shine through the visible environment and in which terror and love, hate and favour, the ghostly and the demonic, the spirit-world and the shining glory of deities are perceptible to the inward eye. It is a world of strangeness, it is uncanny, but it is also familiar and peopled with beings not dissimilar from ourselves. In brief, the world provides the material for religious experience as well as for ordinary perception and technological manipulation.[150]

When we look at Newgrange, we find that in it alone there are 200,000 tonnes of stones and its proportions are immense and quite unnecessary for the marking of the solstices, which can be done just as accurately with standing stones. It took many years of labour for what was then a small population to create Knowth, Dowth and Newgrange, as well as the mounds in the Loughcrew Mountains and many other smaller complexes throughout Ireland. And as burial chambers they were far longer than they needed to be for simple burial – indeed the burial area is often no more than a twentieth of the space.

It seems therefore much more likely that these great temples were built from a deep sense of worship for the clear warm radiance of the sun which drew life from the ground, and the moon who was also the Earth Goddess. All over the world the moon and the earth were closely linked, so much so in the Caribbean that the inhabitants believed them both to have been created out of 'one amorphous substance'.

The vast importance of the sun as a life-giving power must have become apparent to early farmers and indeed its very light would have been worshipped, as it later was in Greece, where Apollo was the Sun-god. Just as the Ice Age people looked into the depths of the caves, so their Stone Age descendants gazed into the skies with the same sense of marvel. The sun must have seemed a divine mightiness, whose absence brought darkness and the sense of threat which many people feel even today when night closes in. Night is the time of fantasy and dream, both containing possible terror, and of the vulnerability of sleep; whereas day, with the sun pouring down from above, is a time of warmth, light and sanctuary. Our feelings have not changed a great deal, even with the use of electricity.

Joseph Campbell has noted the contrast between the night-world of dreams, which are lit from within and seem of a magical nature, with their own arbitrary levels of sense, and the waking world when all the feelings of the night, whether of enchantment or fear, are dispelled by the light. He believes that this waking world must always have been associated with the sun and that the polarity between darkness and light, between mysterious dream-worlds and the guidance of opened eyes, between terror and safety, must be one of the basic structuring principles of human thought.[33]

Measurement, implying a life of order and reason, was one of the outstanding attributes linked to the power of the sun, and the fact that the Stone Age people liked to measure is apparent from their temples. In later times, the laws attached to the power of the sun were developed into the idea that it was a dispenser of cosmic justice. But at that time the sun, as a universal grower of crops, must have given the early farmers belief in it as an almighty god: the lord of light.

That the divine sun was masculine is very possible, although the masculinity of the sun is not so widespread as the femininity of the moon and earth. The earth receives seed and semen-rain from above (women in Australia and Africa still lie in the rain when they want to conceive) and the phallic rays of the sun bring forth plants from the ground. At an even deeper level, the darkness of the earth is related to unknown depths of feeling, to sexual responses, to the womb, whereas the light of the sun is related to conscious life, to individual ambition, to the highest powers such as that of kings, who often take the sign of the sun as their own. The most ancient gender symbol of all, the Chinese yang and yin, shows masculine as white and feminine as black.[85]

THE MOON GODDESS

Yet, for all the feelings of admiration and wonder which the sun inspired, it was to the moon that people in the late Stone Age still dedicated their hearts There are more temples aligned to the moon than to the sun and, as Brennan found out, the sun temples also have their moon alignments. And the symbols of the Goddess, strangely unchanged since Ice Age times, dominate the stone-engraved geometric language of the mound-builders.

It has been pointed out that the amazingly accurate spherical geometry of the Brittany passage graves, the Boyne complex, Avebury and, later, Stonehenge, as well as the abstract patterns of design on the passage grave walls, were probably inspired by the study of the arrangements of the moon, stars and planets.[75] At that time the climate was good and there would have been many clear nights – not to speak of the fact that atmospheric pollution did not exist. Anyone who has visited places far away from cities, such as the Hebrides, will have noticed the wonderful clarity of the light, which seems to bring to life shades of colour never before seen.

The sky must have held an intense fascination for the western world. Shooting stars, comets, the brilliant prominence of a planet such as Venus at certain times of the year must have inspired night after night of star-gazing and calculations. The mathematicians of that era were able to work out, it is now realised, the relationships and harmonies of the heavens and to translate these into their temples of worship, their memory of this knowledge reaching back many thousands of years to the cave-dwellers.

The moon, as the extension of the earth Goddess, became the White Goddess, whose reign extended into later times, and her presence was marked in Newgrange by walls faced with white quartzite, as well as by engraved spirals, concentric circles, lozenges and chevrons. The way in which the long passage itself was aligned to the winter solstice may have represented the birth canal leading to new birth, new life and growth as the sun's rays penetrated down the whole passage. Her womb was the great round chamber, the sacred space at the end of the passage; and her crouching pregnant body was the mound itself (a veritable hill of earth was placed on top of the grave) and the fortunate dead buried in her body would be assured of rebirth.

> The discovery of agriculture radically changed the conception of human existence: it proved to be as frail and ephemeral as the life of plants. Yet, on the other hand, man shared in the cyclical destiny of vegetation: birth, life, death, rebirth; . . . since man's life is like the life of cereals, strength and perenniality become accessible through death. The dead return to the bosom of Mother Earth, with the hope of sharing the destiny of sown seed; but they are also mystically associated with the stone blocks of the burial chambers and consequently become as strong and indestructible as rocks.[61]

THE EYE GODDESS

Throughout Europe in the late Stone Age the Great Goddess was often portrayed by a pair of eyes. The all-seeing eye, the inner eye of the mind, the eye as the link between the mind and the world – any or all might have been intended by this sign. Other geometric shapes are also connected with her, in particular a series of concentric circles with a dot in the middle which may have represented her breast or her womb. In this way artists interpreted the reality of their time, they brought about order and form in nature, and they gave visual expression to the myths by which they lived. The constrained and repetitive patterns of zigzags, lozenges, hooks and circles is a device, like language, to symbolise the physical world, and it is rare for a realistic and natural figure to be found in this art. Gimbutas points out, when she talks about the equally geometric Old European markings, that 'the primary purpose was to transform and spiritualise the body and to surpass the elementary and corporeal'.[70]

There is a feeling of welcome recognition, almost of relief, when a definite pair of eyes can be seen among the myriad angles and curves inscribed on the walls of the passage graves. The most splendid examples come from Iberia where engraved plaques on tombs show round eyes, frequently lashed, with eyebrows above. The farther north she is found the more the Goddess becomes abstract. O.G.S. Crawford, author of *The Eye Goddess*, considers she has 'all gone to pieces'[49] by the time she supposedly reached the French and British passage graves, but we might reflect that the more stylised and abstract eyes show an even greater reverence and celebration of the essential goddess than the plainly obvious ones – just as Greek icon painting is intended to convey the spirit without the individual emotions of the artist getting in the way. But Crawford was writing under the influence of the old archaeology which believed that all culture and civilisation came by way of trade and immigration from the Mediterranean lands.

With new knowledge, provided by radio carbon dating, we could now reverse the development of Crawford's eye symbol and see the Irish eyes as some of the very first, in which case this more abstract form of art is the truer one and the deterioration of understanding came with the unsymbolic and naturalistic eyes of Iberia. It seems to be the case with religions that the more literal they become the less the spirit is revealed. But perhaps we can bridge the great abyss between the old view of the civilised world whose centre was Crete, and the discoveries of Renfrew showing northern France (and Ireland) to be an even earlier civilisation, by agreeing that there must have been much cross-fertilisation of ideas all over Europe, and especially along the Atlantic seaboard, and that such mingling would have included knowledge and beliefs from the Mediterranean world.

Certainly the Eye Goddess penetrated everywhere, from Syracuse to Denmark. In Spain her eyes are always browed and frequently the forehead and cheek are formed by a series of semi-circles. In one design on a pot she looks at us with three eyes, echoing the Indian belief in an 'enlightenment' chakra, the 'third eye'; but it would be wrong to assume that this was the intention. On a kerbstone at Dowth the eyes are engraved on either side of a naturally indented section so that they appear to be prominent, gazing faithfully and for ever at worshippers and newcomers. On a capstone in Newgrange two pairs of eyes, one with brows and the other with a nose, stare out from a multitude of rosettes and other possible eye formations. From a passage grave now sadly broken up, near Liverpool, comes a delightfully merry pair of eyes created by the skilful use of twirling concentric circles in a figure of eight. They are engraved on one of the few stones to be rescued from this figure and show the presence of the Goddess throughout Britain, although the most famous evidence of her presence comes from Folkton Wold in Yorkshire, where three chalk 'drums' were found in a barrow grave – squat cylinders ornamented with eyes which are surrounded by zigzags, triangles and lozenges. Beautifully preserved, they are now in the British Museum and afford an easily viewable glimpse of the Eye Goddess.

But who was the Eye Goddess?

There is no possibility of naming her unless the languages used in the late Stone Age are discovered one day. They may have been inscribed on stone and not yet found – Gimbutas believes that writing was established in eastern Europe by 5000 BCE, perhaps earlier, and it is very likely that the west also had a form of writing. But if it was on perishable material it may have been lost for ever. In its absence, we should take the Eye Goddess as an aspect, a representation, of the Great Goddess. We must study her own language, the language in which she was honoured all over the western world, the language of signs, to tell us about her. From such signs we can know that she was a goddess of fertility, an aspect of the Earth Goddess of the new farming age. She is the natural descendant of the Earth Mother of the Ice Age, but now her role is that of grower of seeds and we can believe that many of the rock symbols signify her pregnancy, which was the pregnancy of the earth. Gimbutas believes that a dot within a lozenge represents the seed within a field – a sown field; and 'a lozenge with a dot or dash at its centre or at the corners must have been a symbolic invocation to secure fertility'.[70] In both eastern and western Europe, the lozenge is one of the most common ideograms. The fertilised and sown field would have been sacred, and since water was essential we should expect to find its equally blessed and sacred sign near the field. Gimbutas believes the zigzag to have been the symbol for running water as it is usually found above the lozenges in most ideograms.[70]

In eastern Europe the eyes of the Eye Goddess are particularly associated with water and it appears that she was the ruler of the force of water. Groups of vertical lines or diagonal parallel lines show the torrents she produced: her eyes are always within or above such lines. Wavy lines also mean water and perhaps are related to a ritual of rain invocation. The Vinča eyelids of eastern Europe have incised parallel lines merging on the nose ridge and the forehead to represent torrents of water pouring from the goddess. In the west the lines encircle the eyes but are likely to be an adaptation of the same theme.

But we should not think of the Eye Goddess as a separate autonomous deity. She was part of the Great Goddess and thus a player in an intricate drama of many roles. The Great Goddess in her command of fertility was undoubtedly responsible for women's pregnancies and the pregnancies of domestic animals and flocks. From the Ice Age she inherited a number of characteristics, one of which must have been the collector of souls, the terrible Goddess of Death (as Kali of India is today), and it may be that the Eye Goddess represented this aspect of her. For the gaze has an unnerving effect.

To be both Goddess of life (through fertility) and also of death may seem a paradox, but perhaps not more so than the similar role of the more modern Father God of the Jews and Christians. The rock engravings, as well as the symbolic forms of the Goddess such as Silbury Hill in Wiltshire, may have been meant to convey just this paradox of 'an entire constellation of meanings' – the fact that life was always changing, that everything created was filled with divine life, that there were sacred patterns which could express and make stronger the creative divinity in matter. 'A true symbol was able to tolerate variety and even contradiction in the messages it received and radiated because, before the Age of Logic (which attempted unsuccessfully to drive away contradiction and to separate opposites) contradiction and paradox were accepted, and acknowledged to be embedded in the nature of things.

'A natural symbol such as the moon (constantly dying and being born) or an underground spring . . . could evoke past, present and future in a single form.'[50]

SILBURY HILL

Between 5000 and 2000 BCE a need to shape the landscape with huge earthworks seems to have swept the Atlantic and North Sea coasts of western Europe. The Boyne Valley complex and Loughcrew are examples of this, but such holy places are so widespread that it can be regarded as a basic religious impulse which dominated western Europe for several thousand years. The earliest of all were in northern France but, as Colin Renfrew points out, we must be careful not to think that they were all the result of a single culture.[142] There are wide variations in the way they were built and some creations, such as the causewayed camps in Britain, do not seem to occur anywhere else.

The causewayed camps are among the very earliest monuments to be built in Britain and their uninspiring name comes from the fact that archaeologists do not know what they were for. They are larger than any other monument (except for the mysterious six-mile long Dorset cursus) and they each cover circular or oval areas of ground of several acres. They are constructed of up to four concentric high banks, with entrances at several places. Maiden Castle in Dorset is a fine example. It was here that one of the rare Goddess figurines was discovered. Although not on high ground, its vast banks and 'causeways' can be seen from many miles away. It carries an aura of immense dignity and power and inspired the writer H.J. Massingham to call it 'the largest and most perfect earthwork in the world'.[117]

These camps are so big that they could only have been built by the communal effort of many people – all that were available, no doubt, because populations were small at that time. At first, archaeologists thought they were ancient livestock corrals for possible market days, but the lack of water near most of them and the fact that some are on the tops of steep hills argue against such a use. Instead, most of the camps show signs of religious and ceremonial uses. Some contained wooden buildings at one time. In others, ritual pits were dug out and have been found to contain skulls and human and animal bones as well as many domestic objects which were probably 'offerings'. The ditches at Windmill Hill were full of animal bones which might have come from ceremonial feasts, although several animals were buried whole indicating a ritual sacrifice. Skulls and human bones might have been taken from tombs for use in religious ceremonies or indeed the corpses might have been exposed, as was then the custom, in the causewayed ditches before their bleached bones were entombed.

Much speculation has arisen about the camps, the only real conclusion being that they were the focus point for a neighbourhood and for public ceremonies. In contrast, the long burial mounds which can be seen in profusion in Dorset, Wiltshire and Hampshire are more likely to have been intimate tombs of small groups or families. These long barrows are built in the same way as the passage graves, but wood was used instead of stone and this has rotted away in most cases, to leave a mere mound.

One of the most extraordinary of all the earthworks in Europe is a solid chalk hill which rises from the Wiltshire plain – Silbury Hill. It is 520 feet in diameter and 130 feet high. It can be seen from miles away and rivets the gaze in exactly the way its creators must have hoped it would. It is the largest man-made mound in Europe and dates back to 2500 BCE. The archaeologist Richard Atkinson has worked out that it would have taken eighteen million man hours to build and the construction must therefore have continued for years, perhaps generations.[5]

The first archaeologists to excavate it were convinced that it must be the tomb of some great king. But no body was inside it and not one of the objects commonly left at burials. Instead they found at the base of it a circular wattle wall, and inside this was a low circular mound of flints in clay. Above this clay core, turf and earth had been stacked so that a cone was created, reaching to the wall, and with its apex in the centre. Michael Dames, the author of *The Silbury Treasure*[51] has pointed out that the measurements of this cone are exactly the same as the sanctuary hut in nearby Avebury. And Richard Atkinson discovered that the central clay base mound lies precisely under the centre of the flat top of the hill.

Michael Dames has demonstrated through photograph and description that one of the uses of this tiered chalk hill with its central cone was as a solid eye gazing up to the sky. At nearby Durrington Walls, a causewayed camp bounded by six concentric circles, the Eye Goddess is shown on pottery discovered there. Eyes made up of concentric circles gaze out from four different pots and 'pot and building offer two views of the one reality'. Dames believes that at Silbury 'the dark hidden eye was expanded, using concentric and radial chalk walling, to turn the entire hill into a fat treatment of the oculi motif, appropriate for harvest'.[51]

It appears that in the late Stone Age the Goddess might have come to represent a trinity of sun, moon and earth, with the Eye representing one of her functions. It is possible that the sun was given some masculine characteristics but this did not mean that he was not part of the Goddess, for her image frequently contains a phallus. In Somerset, a wooden figurine was found which has been carbon dated to 3000 BCE. It has both breasts and a phallus and had been placed in a peg to point it upside down towards the earth. 'Divine bisexuality stresses her absolute power,' says Gimbutas.[70] In the south-east perimeter of the Silbury mound, a perforated stone of hard grey schist was found. It was two inches long and half an inch thick and was 'shaped like the long goddess of a thousand schist idols, and *used as a sickle sharpener*. This object makes the point that Neolithic art was intended to present agricultural processes and technology in terms of the superhuman body.'[51] And, too, that most widespread and ancient of all Goddess symbols, a pair of ox horns, was found embedded in the earth of Silbury Hill.

But it is perhaps the relationship of Silbury with its surroundings that bears out Dames's belief that 'Silbury is the Great goddess pregnant',[51] her womb the cone found inside her, her body the mound itself. For the earth for the mound was quarried around her and the pit then filled with water as an artificial lake to delineate the rest of her body. In this way the Goddess can be symbolised as both eye and womb in one, and the eye-womb is perhaps the real meaning of the sets of concentric circles in the passage graves.

Because of the relationship of Silbury and the nearby ancient henge of Avebury, Dames believes that Silbury was aligned to both sun and moon and that its most important role was at harvest time. It was a harvest hill. And the combination of harvest hills and henges has been noted in other places such as Arbor Low in Derbyshire and Knowlton in Dorset.

'In winter, the Harvest Mother does not vanish from but *into* the earth, into the bone mound, there to receive the dead. For this purpose her body, although preserving the squatting pregnant posture, was made suitably hollow.'[51] Dames briefly lists the components which made up her presence, some of which (6, 8 and 9) refer to objects found inside her:

the pregnant seated goddess
the goddess half buried in the ground
the Eye Goddess, supreme intelligence
the White Mountain in the primordial water
the cosmic egg
sickle, grain and cornstook
the throne

the stag
the umbilical snakes
mother and child
woman with phallus – the androgynous being
the spinning and weaving goddess.[51]

The stag refers to antlers found within the mound and the snakes refer to a pair of coiling rope-strands made up of grass which were laid on the floor of the cone.

A STONE AGE CATHEDRAL

Nearby Avebury was built, it is thought, at the same time as Silbury and is the greatest of the nine hundred British stone circles. A hundred huge sarsen stones, only some of which remain, once stood within an encircling bank some fifty feet in height. Inside this circle were built two inner circles, one north and one south. Two avenues of stones once led into these circles. One is entirely lost but the other mostly survives. This, the West Kennett Avenue, goes to the Sanctuary on Overton Hill – and although most of the Sanctuary was destroyed in the eighteenth century, it is still possible to see not only a circle of stones but also a much older circle of postholes for what was once a timber roundhouse.

Before the Sanctuary and Avebury were both largely destroyed, the eighteenth-century antiquarian William Stukeley made detailed engravings of the whole complex. From these engravings it can be seen that the lost avenue formed a serpentine shape when it entered into the vast womb of Avebury. The remaining West Kennett Avenue is made up of alternating fat and thin stones – which can be interpreted as male and female, or as the virgin and pregnant Goddess. The male and female theory is a little more likely as the fat stones are frequently hewn into a diamond shape, thought to be the ideogram of the Goddess, leaving the thinner, erect ones as males.

Even though much of Avebury was destroyed, both by the church and by the fearful work of a local farmer, 'Stonekiller' Robinson, who hired gangs of men to smash and burn the stones in the eighteenth century, enough is left to make it a 'cathedral' of the late Stone Age. Part of the village of Avebury lies within the circles and the cottages themselves seem to give the site a feeling of harmony between man and the sacred, which is not often found. It is an exceptionally serene and beautiful place, full of nuances of rising and falling ground, shadows from the great stones, softly rounded bank and ancient trees, grazing sheep and singing larks. It is a place implicit with being, its subtle strength sustaining and welcoming the visitor.

It can be seen as part of a reverent arrangement of monuments, all of which celebrate the Goddess in her different modes. Silbury is the Harvest Goddess, who gives birth and who also retreats at death; West Kennett, the burial passage, is her grave and also the place of her rebirth; and Avebury is the Goddess as bride and also the temple where she will conceive. The ancient symbols of the Goddess and her male god-self can be found in the archetypal sexual imagery of the snake as phallus entering along the line of the now extinct Beckhampton Avenue and meeting in the open vulva of the south circle the serpentine line of fat and thin stones coming from the Overton Sanctuary.[50]

A visit to this group of temples gives a wonderful sense of the relationship between one site and another, how each was probably venerated at a different time of year, and how they present the complete Goddess by bringing together all her functions and moods.

DEATH AND SACRIFICE

Standing on the green wall of Avebury, or on Silbury Hill, it is easy to see the nearby long stone-lined passage grave of West Kennett. Dames believes that when the Silbury goddess retreated into the underworld after the harvest, the next great event in the drama of the year was that of the dying world, the beginning of winter, on the quarter day midway between the autumn equinox and the winter solstice. This would be signified by death itself within the passage grave, and almost certainly dead people would be placed there at that time. And since the moon played a bigger role than the sun in the agricultural calendar and in the hearts of the people, the ritual ceremonies would have taken place on a night of blackness when the moon too was dead.

Was somebody sacrificed for the purpose of appeasing the

dying Mother? It is very likely. In the nearby Sanctuary at Avebury, a circular shaft pointed to the burial of a boy of fourteen, whose body was crouched in the pre-birth position with arms crossed and hands enfolding his face. He lay on his right side, facing east, and a pot was between his knees. All his bones had been broken and the bones of a young ox had been placed on top of his body, as well as a bored horn amulet in the stylised shape of the Goddess. Joseph Campbell reminds us that sacrifices were often 'fresh enactments, here and now, of the god's own sacrifice in the beginning, through which he, she or it became incarnate in the world process'.[35] Rebirth would be assured for the one who was sacrificed and the powers of life renewed for all who took part in the ceremony.

THE WHITE GODDESS

The building of the great temples – and Avebury alone covers twenty-eight acres – can be seen as the making of an act of union with the creator of the cosmos. For the creator might well have been envisaged as having the dimensions of the universe itself – and so any temple built for it should be correspondingly mighty. The temple symbolised, as did the cave paintings of the Ice Age, a belief in the integrated harmony of the spiritual and the material, that the one expresses the other and they can never be divided. What more natural than to build a temple in the actual shape of the Goddess? Or, indeed, of the god who was both her lover and herself, for the remains of a gigantic temple some hundred yards long and shaped like a phallus have recently been discovered in Gloucestershire.

Dames believes that chalk was deliberately used to embody a White Goddess, for the chalk uplands of Wessex form one of the greatest European centres for her worship. We know from many symbols that the Goddess was associated from early times with the clear light of the full moon – and the white chalk must have suggested itself as moon-material on earth. Quartzite faced the walls at Newgrange to create a white effect. White has come down to us even today as the colour for a bride, and although it is nowadays associated with an emphasis on purity its origin may perhaps be more ancient, going back to the time when every newly bedded girl was herself the embodiment of the Goddess and perhaps wore white at her entry into womanhood (it is possible that a form of marriage took place at that time).

And, as Dames points out, the smooth undulating hills themselves resembled the Goddess, 'for there people of the New Stone Age could walk on the torso of the divinity, explore her breasts, her armpits, the space between her thighs, or run the endless swell and ripple of her back for mile after mile, all the way from Dorset to East Anglia, or from Kent to the Yorkshire Wolds.'[50]

The anthropologist Lévi-Strauss tells us that people in the late Stone Age knew a great ambition to symbolise the divine in earth and rock 'such as humanity has never again seen equalled', and they believed implicitly that the 'solid earth from which they carved the symbol and the Goddess herself were one and the same'.[60]

The cosmic power of the earth would have been seen as continually present, never ceasing, and men and women must have felt confidence that they were capable of co-operating in such creation, both with their work and in their union (the act of sexual union would never have been regarded as merely erotic). And to move upon the Goddess and farm upon her body as she revealed herself in hill and vale was to be part of both time and timelessness, matter and spirit.

CHAPTER FIVE
A religion of stone

Between the years of 2700 and 1200 BCE, a great surge of activity created most of the stone circles and rows of stones that can still be seen today. It is a time which historians have found difficult to decipher. Until quite recently it was believed that western Europe was invaded by a race of round-headed, rather stocky people from the Rhineland, who brought with them an attractive way of making pots or 'beakers'. The original peoples who had built the passage graves were in the main long-headed and tall and their graves were the communal long barrows, whereas the round-heads built small round barrows within which a single person was buried. They earned the title of the Beaker people because, with every corpse, a beaker was found which had probably contained a herb-flavoured alcoholic beverage. Ornaments, clothing and weapons were also put with the body, but the beaker stood out as the mark of a particular burial rite. Both sexes qualified for such burials and so it is assumed that it was not a warrior burial class which was given the honour of a mound. Touchingly, in the instances where a mother and baby were buried together, the baby was supplied with a baby-sized beaker.[78]

Earlier historians called the arrival of the Beaker people an 'invasion' but in fact there is not much evidence to support this. Burial practices were never standardised in the west and although it does appear that the long barrows up to about 3000 BCE were built by long-headed people and that in the following centuries they gave way to round mounds where round-headed people were buried, there is no precision about this. Long-headed people have been found with beakers and sometimes both long- and round-head have shared the same grave.

Perhaps the nearest we can come to the truth is to say that there were a number of slightly different looking people in the west during this millennium and that they practised various death and burial rites. They seem to have got on well together, and it was only towards the end of this era when good land was scarcer that feuds began.

The Beaker people have always been associated with the introduction of bronze tools – the first metal – and we can see this as taking place over a number of centuries. Stone implements continued to be made for a long time while the metal technology was developing. It began with the working of copper and gold, although gold was much rarer. But while simple objects can be made from copper by the use of an ordinary fire, anything subjected to heavy use needs melting to a very high temperature in special kilns and furnaces. The understanding of how to make these kilns probably came from central Europe, but the big turning point in the whole metal industry arrived when the discovery was made that tin added to copper (and tin could be melted at much lower temperatures) resulted in a very tough metal indeed – bronze.

CIRCLES OF SACRED SPACE

Whatever religion the Beaker people had of their own (and their ritual burials indicate a strong belief in an afterlife, or rebirth), there seems to have been a general acceptance of each other's beliefs in the new mixed communities, and a grafting of new ideas on to old. The long barrows and passage graves were probably going out of use before the Beaker cult became established, but it appears that the same celebratory passion for building vast monuments continued and came to be realised in the great ritual enclosures and avenues of Stonehenge and the Brittany complexes.

Indeed, stone circles had long been used for encircling and defining a sacred space, such as Newgrange and Avebury. But with the advent of the Beaker people the population grew and the labour of moving the big stones was no longer such a problem. Certainly a new spurt of building seems to have taken place at the time of the new round mounds.

Many books have been written about the most famous of all the circles, Stonehenge, but since it is the most magnificent of its kind in the west it is worth briefly going over old ground. It was built in three stages. Stonehenge I consisted of a ring of fifty-six holes, some including bones and some not, surrounded by a six-foot earthen wall and constructed about 2800 BCE. The circular bank had one entrance at the north-east. It is the holes which have aroused most interest, since apparently as soon as they were made they were filled up with white chalk and were never used for holding posts or stones. Yet they were set out with great accuracy around a circumference of which the diameter was 284 feet – and the biggest error in spacing was a mere twenty-one inches.[172] Archaeologists have concluded that the mathematicians of the early Bronze Age must have used geometrical instruments which have not yet been recognised as such – or, perhaps, if they were made of wood, will never be found. Nevertheless, a precise measurement common to all the megaliths of north-western Europe has been discovered. This is the 'megalithic yard', a length of 2.72 feet. This 'yard' was used to lay out complex circles and avenues – a mark of unusual technical ability in a society which possessed no written communication that we know of.[187]

The holes (called Aubrey holes after John Aubrey who discovered and recorded in the seventeenth century) are thought now to be markers for the phases of the moon. They show where the winter moon rose over a 56-year period which allows for all its different positions in its 18.61-year cycle. Since the fertility symbol of a pair of ox horns was dug up in the central area of Stonehenge, it is now believed that the original intention was a moon observatory dedicated to the Moon or Mother Goddess, and that this concept changed over the course of time to a sun observatory. The Aubrey holes were undoubtedly a moon feature. Not only were they an accurate calculator of its phases, but their chalk-white appearance and the fact that many of them contained skulls and bones demonstrate, in the symbolism of that time, adoration of the moon as Goddess.

The building of Stonehenge II took place some five hundred years later. Eighty-two 'bluestones', each of them weighing over four tons, were brought along rivers and over land from the Prescelly Mountains of West Wales, some 240 miles away.[112] Such a feat has always staggered archaeologists. Once more the question is: why go to the trouble of bringing such vast stones over such a distance when others could have been found near at hand? There is no trace of the bluestones now, but evidence has shown that they were originally arranged in a circle of sixty, with two horseshoes inside the circle.

It might be that bluestone was valued as having some holy power. Ritual pieces were put at the bottom of later shafts at Stonehenge, chips were found in burials and it was also used for the highly polished stone axes. It may well be that its particular location in the high Prescelly Mountains was itself regarded as holy.[4] Sacred mountains are common to mankind, their awe-inspiring presence diminishing everyday concerns and lifting the spirit towards another reality. It seems very likely that Bronze Age people, with their senses keenly attuned to the physical universe of colour and form, believed that the blue western mountains represented an entrance to the afterworld.

Stonehenge III was built at about 1700 BCE. The bluestones were removed and carefully preserved while seventy-seven gigantic sarsen stones, each weighing on average 26 tons, were dragged from outcrops some twenty miles away. Even today such an enterprise would be regarded as fraught with difficulty and when we think of the magnitude of that undertaking in terms of ropes, wooden rollers and muscle, we can only believe that the greatest religious fervour must have inspired it. For not only were the stones brought to the site, they then had to be positioned with precise accuracy according to the heavens – for Stonehenge was an astronomical observatory as well as other things. The stones were then dressed and pounded with mauls and rubbed smooth, their sides fluted. Then they were pushed and pulled into their holes, some of them weighing forty tons or more. The lintels which crossed from the top of one stone to another were then lowered. These lintels were extremely heavy stone slabs which had been tongued and grooved, mortised and tendoned, rebated and curved to the line of the circle. They had to be levered up from the ground and placed precisely in position. After this the bluestones were put back within the circle.

Thousands of words have been written about the astronomical purpose of Stonehenge as a remarkable central observatory for studying the sun, moon and stars. With the publication of *Stonehenge Decoded* by G.S. Hawkins,[86] as well as the study of Stonehenge by the astronomer Fred Hoyle,[92] there can now be no doubt that Bronze Age interest in the sky was both intense and technically advanced. But it is easy to be carried away by the sheer mathematics involved so that other explanations of the circle's purpose fade into the background. It is true that the marvel of the heavens has inspired man's observation for untold centuries but why were the bluestones brought from Wales and why were the mammoth sarsens erected? They were unnecessary for a competent observatory; a wooden building would have done as well.

We have to turn to deeper beliefs if we are to come to any real appreciation of Stonehenge – or, indeed, of all the other stone circles scattered over western Europe. For instance, the understanding of cosmic time lends itself to a *circular cycle*, particularly within the organic framework of agriculture where the rhythm of birth, death and rebirth appears as a round. The ancient Chinese symbol for existence was a circle, empty in the middle – for, like the continuation of the life-force itself, a circle has no ending. It is both infinite and total and its void centre was thought to represent the transcendent core of existence. We can easily believe that the sacred space within a circle might have represented the 'centre of the world'. According to Eliade, the 'centre of the world' is a consecrated area, made holy by the prayers and rituals which take place in it, 'for it is there that communication with superhuman beings is effected'.[3]

Bronze Age man almost certainly had a capacity for experiencing every moment of his life as having a transcendent as well as an ordinary meaning. So perhaps the builders of the stone circles hoped to reveal the understanding of that eternal cycle of interdependence and interaction which makes up the universe. Certainly it could be said that humanity became obsessed with stone. Throughout the world stone was the material of reverent magic so that, with strange synchronicity, monuments were created not only in Europe but also in Asia, South America and Australia. Stone itself was a symbol of some ideal or quality which we perhaps will never understand; it may have given forth a luminosity which our senses are too dull to receive, although the feel of rock – of limestone or granite – is strangely attractive to our hands even today. The fact that stones were thought to be connected with humankind itself is shown by the Indo-European word 'man' which is the same as stone. Thus in Celtic a menhir is a standing stone, a dolmen a table stone.[122]

It may also be that

> megalithic man needed to know about eclipses, solstices, equinoxes, and high geometry because, in some way that we do not now understand he felt that these were vital to the proper working of the stones. He wasn't just building observatories, although they could be used as these. The reverse was more important; he was constantly experimenting, placing all his stones so that at certain key moments in the rhythms of the cosmos, his magical stones were imbued with a supernatural energy that renewed and enhanced life on earth. . . . If we tried to create a stone circle today we wouldn't know how to make it work. A dowser could find us a site with the right underground forces, or where there had once been a circle; an archeologist could excavate and show us the original position of the stones; an astronomer could show us where to replace them so as to take account of the changed conditions in the heavens; and a geologist could take us to the right sort of rocks. But even if a power might then be generated, it would be a different sort of power.[87]

Another purpose for the circles might have been to 'empower' – to enable the person entering the circle to feel a heightened sense of holiness, of the power to break through to another level of existence. To be empowered is to feel oneself in touch with greatness, with a sacred presence, from which one receives the ability to love and serve. Stonehenge nowadays has dismally fallen into such a tourist-beleaguered condition that few could feel such a sensation there, especially as people are now no longer allowed within the circle. But when it was first finished it must have been regarded as the greatest sanctuary and holy powerhouse of the western world – indeed of the world itself, for even Delphi and the Pyramids are of a later date.

Stone circles everywhere were almost certainly believed to be sacred spaces where non-human power could be concentrated and received. In an experiment called the Dragon project,[145] a number of scientists and other investigators got together to 'finally' unravel the mystery of the stone circles. They decided to study both radioactivity and ultrasound emitted from the stones. Unusual radiation levels in the circles had been reported, but ultrasound had not really been considered until a piece of news came in from a naturalist, a student of bats, whose equipment had suddenly picked up ultrasonic sound from a standing stone.

The Rollright Stone Circle in Oxfordshire was chosen as the sample. Many reasons contributed, such as its availability and the fact that it is steeped in the legends often associated with stone circles – that the stones cannot be counted, that they move about at night, and that they have curative properties. The group of scientists began their operation in October on one very early morning before dawn. The leader, Don Robins, said that he felt very foolish with his recording device in the dew-drenched grey light and had decided to tell anyone who came along that he was a tourist with an unusual transistor. But just half an hour before sunrise, 'the Kingstone suddenly sprang to life, emitting a regular signal which was neither the rhythm of his heart, the rustle of the undergrowth, or some errant radio transmission. It was a glorious moment. The signals lasted through the dawn, gradually fading as the sun climbed the sky.'[145]

Such a response led the scientists to monitor other sites and to devise more sophisticated screening so that they could rule out all other sources of sound. They discovered that the stones alone were responsible. At the same time the Geiger counter was showing unusual levels of radioactivity within the circles.

A decision had to be made whether to drop the whole experiment or carry it on to the point where enough evidence was available to 'satisfy the demands of scientific respectability and prove that there was a genuine scientific phenomenon at the circles'. The decision was taken to go ahead and this is what they found:

> At the time of the equinoxes – March and October – the stones emit regular ultrasonic signals. It happens around dawn whether or not the sun is visible and quite independently of weather conditions. As the year draws on towards the solstices, the signals fade away.
>
> But stranger by far, from time to time, the stones create an ultrasonic barrier. A cone of silence on the hillside. 'This is the weirdest thing. You always have a background of ultrasound in the country – the movements of grasses, leaves rustling, even your own clothing. It all registers. But one morning, as we moved in and out of the circle monitoring the levels, suddenly we found that there was complete ultrasonic

silence inside the circle. Our first thoughts were that it was an instrument malfunction. Then we walked through the gap in the stones and there was sound. Inside, silence – outside, normal background levels.'[145]

At the same time the Geiger counters were picking up radioactivity of unusual intensity between the Kingstone, an outlying stone at the top of a steep slope, and the circle. Yet inside the circle the readings were much lower. One of the scientists took infrared photographs of the Kingstone and to everyone's astonishment they showed a light mist around it and a ray beaming upwards from its top.

Robins was worried for his scientific reputation by the implications of this discovery. 'What we seem to have found,' he explained, 'are refuges. The stones shield the interior of the circle from certain energy fields. They seem to exclude cosmic radiation too, and that implies spherical shelter. It is as though the circles created holes in the landscape.'[145]

Other circles all over Britain and Ireland were investigated and in the end they decided to risk their reputations and publish their findings in *New Scientist*. To Robins's relief, 'Amazingly the archaeologists were not too aghast.'[145] He added that scientists are more relaxed about the inexplicable these days.

Quite unknown to him, a retired BBC engineer, Charles Brooker, had already made several electromagnetic scans of the Rollright circle with a portable magnometer. He had found a seven-ring spiral of magnetic intensity inside the circle, and when he read Robins's article he followed it with one of his own, also in *New Scientist*. He too had come to the conclusion that the circles form magnetic refuges – although from what is anybody's guess. It was pointed out that ultrasonic sound is used nowadays to heal damaged tissue and improve seed germination, and this may be the origin of the folk tales about healing and fertility powers within the circles.

Such a report brings up the whole matter of attunement to the powers of the universe. Were our ancestors so much better attuned than we are today to the vibrations of the earth and the atmosphere that they understood – even if not academically – much of what we are discovering with machines? Was the atmosphere so much purer that they could in fact *see* the mist around the

Kingstone and the beam of light? Were the circles placed to accord with certain natural laws of the universe to which they responded but to which we are now insensitive? The ancient Chinese had an understanding of how to build in accord with the directions of wind and water and lines of the earth. They called it *feng shui*, and regarded it as an essential intuition for harmonious building. Perhaps such an intuition is innate to man but nowadays is blunted through lack of use in our overcrowded and industrialised countries.

What might be said about the circles with some credibility is that the empty centre is a place where finely attuned senses may become aware of an unusual feeling of clarity. The shielded nature of that inner space may have represented the spirit of man at one with the transcendent. Perhaps, like a mandala, it was meant to be a diagram of the way things are – the inmost beingness at the still and silent centre and the outer body of stones vibrating with electromagnetic activity. 'The ground of the mind and the ground of God are one sole essential being,'[9] said Eckhart, and the centre of the circle was perhaps the place where that could be experienced.

But we should not forget the circle as a symbol of the womb – which would not in those days have been regarded as interfering in any way with its other purposes. Many stone circles are not in fact circles but egg-shaped, or oval. Geometrically they are just as correct in the alignment of the stones, but the function in at least the egg-shaped ones would have been fertility, with ritual offerings and worship within the circle or around it. All its purposes, spiritual and material, would have been seen as interacting and interweaving, and the intellectual distinctions we might make between one function and another would then have seemed irrelevant.

THE SHAPE OF THE STONES

The stones themselves, especially in a place like Stanton Drew – a rather neglected great circle behind a farm in Somerset – are often so vast and impressive that a feeling of 'source-power' seems to emanate from them. Stanton Drew was once a great vital centre with three circles, the main one being the second largest in

England. But now many of the huge stones have fallen and lie remote from each other, so that the feeling of a circle barely exists. Yet some of the individual stones have a strong presence of their own, especially the standing ones, which tower above the person. One or two seem to have been hewn to a particular shape, rather like giant axes. This may indeed be so, since axes seem to have been ritually associated with circles and several archaeologists speak of an 'axe-cult'. Stone axes have been found in and near Avebury and are also carved on to the stones at Stonehenge. All over north-west Europe they have been found ritually buried with bodies and there is some possibility that they were connected with a god of storm and thunder, although the double-headed axe was also a Goddess symbol in eastern Europe. They played a mysterious role. Many were polished to a high degree and were quite fragile, so were used perhaps in sacred ceremonies. Some evidence links them with a god of the sun rather than storm and if this were the case then their presence at Stonehenge, which was for at least some of the time a temple of the sun, is explained. Stanton Drew is thought to have been a sun temple also. Strangely enough, some of the earliest tools from far-off Neanderthal times are small heart-shaped, unfunctional axes, looking as though they had served a ritual purpose. This symbol, as with many others, was reborn again and again.

A strange circumstance, to which little attention has been paid by archaeologists, is the fact that all the stone circles, avenues and individual stones stand out most clearly from their surroundings *when seen from above*. Close to, their impressiveness is greatly diminished, whereas seen from the sky they are staggering. This does not mean they were built to assist the landing of UFOs. But it could mean that man saw the earth as part of the vast solar system and the monuments were built for the gaze of sun, moon and stars. Undoubtedly the moon was a goddess, the sun almost certainly a deity too, and very likely the larger stars and planets were endowed with deity status. If these were the visible gods, with some great invisible presence pervading both them and all creation, it is to the sky that man would have directed his worship, no doubt believing that all he did was seen from above (as fundamentalist Christians still believe today). It would have been a tremendous act of homage to build a structure aligned to the heavenly bodies, as Stonehenge is, and to build it in such a way that seen from the sky it would be more significant than seen from the ground. Readers may remember a 'Horizon' television programme about the prehistoric Nazca Indians of Peru, who made immense pictograms for the gods by clearing lines on a stone-covered plain so that 'drawings' appeared. The programme showed a number of shapes and creatures created in this way, but they could only be distinguished *from the air*. At ground level the lines were totally meaningless and thus invisible.

Perhaps the continuance of the feeling that sun, moon and stars were the rulers of the world – or were rulers as appendages of a great Presence – was the cause of the later carvings in chalk of the sky-tilted Cerne Abbas giant and the White Horse of Uffington, for seen from ground level their impact is much diminished.[68]

If the great monuments were sky-turned, we can only be astonished at the ingenuity and mathematical understanding of the builders. And indeed the accuracy with which Stonehenge was built is quite uncanny, particularly as it is the only building of its sort in western Europe. With its morticed and tongued joinery, the great sarsen circle deviates by less than four inches from true circumference. Belief that a form of plumbline or setsquare was used is now strong. Stonehenge alone rules out the idea that the west was in any sense 'backward', for the techniques employed there were only rivalled in later years by Egypt and Greece.

AVENUES AND SOLITARY STONES

At Carnac, in Brittany, eleven lines of standing stones, numbering 1099, depart from a grand stone circle in a gentle course to the north-east, the size of the stones decreasing as they go. Eventually they lead to a stone ring half a mile away. A little distance farther on they begin again from what was probably the site of another circle, but which has now become a car park. They run down into a valley and then stretch away east and west, line after line, even marching over the top of a long earth barrow. When excavated in 1922, this barrow contained arrangements of small stones, but there were no human remains. A great solitary stone stood on top of it, oriented to a different direction than the avenues. Below ground level, the excavators found five wavy lines carved near the base of this stone. Close by were five small axes, well polished.

The whole Carnac complex – for there are other alignments, avenues and circles – creates an instant picture of long processions under the soft clouds of Brittany, with music and chanting and the expectation of communion with the Goddess in that final barrow; or perhaps in the strange 'square' of stones nearby – although not all of the stone avenues coincide here. The whole district of Carnac and the nearby Gulf of Morbihan was one of the religious centres of the western world. The Gulf is full of small islands. One in particular has a sweeping view of all the others and on it is the great burial mound of Gavrinis. Within the stone passage grave every inch of available wall is covered by the dazzling designs familiar from Newgrange, although here the axe theme is even more important. And here, too, serpents with small bulging heads herald the Goddess. One unusual feature is a deep round groove cut into the stone horizontally, so that a visitor can put an arm into a deep recess. Unusual grooves, although only on the surface and oblong in shape, appear also in Dartmoor on two major stones at the beginning of parallel rows.

Such avenues bring to mind a ritualistic splendour and fervour in worship which has long since departed from most of the west. But what of the single standing stones, so many of which enhance the countryside? One tall stone, or sometimes a pair, can be found in almost every neighbourhood. Eliade suggests that such a stone might represent the actual body of a person, to be there for eternity, so that descendants might go back to receive virtues from the dead ancestor[3] in which case, our present practice of marking a grave with a stone might have descended from this time. But it is possible too that the stones represent the Goddess and her male self. The shape of many of the stones is unquestionably phallic. Near Madron in Cornwall, two such phallic stones stand beside a large circular stone through which a round hole has been carved out. The hole is so big that a person can go through it. Originally these stones stood in a triangle, the classic ideogram for the female pubic region. It is believed that the holed stone might once have formed the entrance to a burial chamber, the womb-tomb of the Goddess. One authority on local customs thinks that the permanently rigid phallic shape seems to signify belief in a permanent spirit resident in the stones: 'Can we take this a step further and suggest that the stones were not only symbols, but actual tools, carefully placed for very good reasons? They may have actually been huge stone phalluses, capable of accumulating natural energy and directing it into the earth – impregnating and fertilising the Earth Mother.'[23] A stone phallic erection seems to have been a universal symbol, found in other countries also, such as the lingam of Hindu India.

ASTRONOMER PRIESTS

The change to stone circles and standing stones from earthen long barrows and passage graves may have had profound implications of a religious nature. To create Stonehenge and Avebury or the Carnac complex whole communities must have laboured for years. Who directed them? Who first had the vision of the completed monuments? Was it an inspired vision which was shared by everybody, or was there in existence a group of seer-priests, with astronomical and mathematical knowledge, who organised the work of the many?

Euan MacKie, author of *Science and Society in Prehistoric Britain*,[112] believes that there was indeed a strong priestly elite in the late Stone and early Bronze Ages. They were probably the predecessors of the druids and merged imperceptibly with them later on. In MacKie's view, the great wooden roundhouses of the first henges – built before stone replaced them – provide evidence for religious centres which were permanently occupied by priests and their servers and followers. In places such as Skara Brae in Mainland Orkney, where timber was scarce, they lived in stone rather than wooden houses, and these are still standing. Such houses have indeed revealed a higher standard of living than one would expect in that place and at that time. There was furniture in the form of stone tables, shelves and beds (on which straw and woven materials would have been laid). It is not thought that such standards would have been common to everyone.

Other evidence comes from the fact that the people who lived in the roundhouses apparently ate pork when everyone else ate beef. There is little sign of butchering or of bread-making inside the houses, so perhaps food was brought in ready-made. With such special treatment there seems to be confirmation of MacKie's belief that priests occupied these specially built houses, keeping alive the long-acquired knowledge of astronomy and mathematics, while the rest of the people clothed and fed them and followed their guidance. A henge-house of this sort was almost invariably close to a great circle-sanctuary, with avenues leading between for priest-led processions.

Critics of this theory point out that a great deal of geometric and astronomical data would have had to be recorded and no such records have ever been discovered – or, we might say, recognised. Certainly the amazing fact, verified from Newgrange and Stonehenge, that prehistoric man had accurately estimated the cycle of the moon at 18.6 months, means that he must have spent years in continual observation. But the ancient way of recording knowledge was by ritual repetition or chanting, and if we can follow MacKie in envisaging a group of astronomer-priests as they taught schools of novices, we may see an oral tradition as the clue to the building of Stonehenge and other places – particularly as such an oral tradition was a characteristic of the early Celts, who were perhaps already appearing on the scene.

There is also a recording device and a kind of language in the placing of the stones themselves, not to speak of all the myriad engravings carved on them. Notched wood, which has now disintegrated, might also have been used; or perhaps the cup and ring marks carved on rocks, which are so common all over Europe and occur in such abundance that more than one archaeologist has wondered if they represented the stars.

Were the priest-astronomers, if they existed, men or women? The question does not seem to have occurred to MacKie and those who agree with his theories. This is largely because of the eclipse of women during the last 2000 years, so that the possibility that they would have had any status does not even come into the minds of male historians. But without any need to adopt a feminist stance, we should recognise that in the period we are studying it is likely that women were highly revered as direct manifestations of the Goddess; and although there is no actual evidence, it is probable that society tended to be matriarchal. Women's minds are inherently as competent as men's and given the conditions of priestesshood there seems to be no reason why women rather than men, or perhaps both men and women, could not have been the wisdom-sources, the astronomers, the mathematicians and the spiritual leaders.

THE STONE AGE ENDS

In the later Bronze Age, and particularly after the discovery of iron, the spirit of western humanity seems to have gone into a decline. In these last chapters we have witnessed a society which was innately peaceful. True, there were local skirmishes as some burials have revealed, and true, it is almost certain that humans as well as animals were used in ritual sacrifices. But the overall picture is one of co-operation in the building of the monuments and harmony with regard to burying the dead.

Theirs was an intensely personalised world – one which is almost unimaginable today – in which every rock and tree, even every tool, would have had its own spirit, sometimes malign, sometimes beneficent. In such a world nothing was ever meaningless. But with the abandonment of stone for the increasing use of metal, something changed in people's hearts. After the final stage in the building of Stonehenge, about 1700 BCE, the fervour for the spectacular spiritual power-house began to evaporate. New burial customs arose, such as cremation, with the bones placed in an urn within a mound. The erecting of solitary standing stones continued for several centuries after the circles had ceased to be built, but even though the old ways might still have exerted some influence the cutting edge of metal was to be their undoing. Sharp swords replaced stone axes, and arrows came to be tipped with barbed metal points.[154] The killing time was beginning. It is fitting to close this chapter with a question, one which is put by Philip van Doren Stern in his book *Prehistoric Europe*:

> The major question about the new state of being that mankind was rapidly approaching . . . is: in ultimate values was it worth the cost? Is all that has resulted from it – our advanced culture, our scientific achievements, our amazingly complex technology, our enormously increased body of knowledge, our good health, our comfort, our luxury – worth the turmoil, anguish, bloodshed, cruelty, and wholesale murder that are part of the price we have had to pay – and are still paying – for these supposed gains?
>
> The question must be asked in any discussion of man's presumed progress from animal existence to what we call

civilisation. And it must be asked here, for man was now about to go from what seems to have been a fairly simple outdoor food-gathering and food-growing life to a new kind of existence in crowded communities that have always been at war with each other. That the human race moved forward is certain, but whether or not it went on to a condition that was better than what it had been is a matter that each person must answer for himself. Perhaps there are no definite answers, perhaps there never were and never will be, but this eternal question is the key to all enquiries into the greatness, the glory, and the incredible nastiness of man's career upon the earth he has ravaged.[154]

CHAPTER SIX
Creation and imagination: the Celts

Before the end of the Bronze Age a class system had begun to operate in western Europe. Rich chieftains were buried with golden ornaments and their earthen fortresses appeared on many hilltops. The people were separating into frequently warring tribes and by 1400 BCE the noble common purpose which had created Avebury and Stonehenge, when men and women dedicated themselves to great communal tasks, appears to have evaporated.

Most of the causewayed camps were turned into hillforts and the bigger ones, such as Maiden Castle, grew into packed cities within their great walls and ditches. A complicated political system seems to have existed of warlike tribal chieftains whose realms were fairly extensive. In Britain particularly, where the hillforts jostle each other around the great causewayed power centres, it seems likely that barons and lesser nobles fortified themselves with earthen walls and defended homesteads, while the kings or chiefs dwelt in grander style in minor fortified cities.

The nature of the people was undergoing inevitable change. Instead of a peaceable community, strongly attuned to the cosmic laws of being and the magnetic forces of the earth, the hillforts seem to tell us of a newly insecure and fractious society in which individual greed and ego were becoming dominant. We can know quite a bit about what the people looked like and what they wore and ate from the preserved bodies recovered from Danish bogs. We know that a number of cereals were used to make bread and that it and meat were the staple foods. The men wore woollen tunics and capes, with close caps, while the women wore decorated wollen tunics, bonnets, girdles and tassels, and hairnets.

This uneasy society came to be joined – as early perhaps as 2000 BCE – by new waves of settlers, the Celts; or one should say, by Celtic-speaking immigrants, for the Celts were never a very unified nation but rather were a collection of volatile tribes with a taste for trade and art. 'Since the Celts were always in a minority and did not, strictly speaking, constitute a single Celtic race, the Celtic world was primarily a conglomeration of different nations under a Celtic elite, the indigenous peoples being first enslaved and then fused together by a common Celtic language, civilisation and religion.'[115] They brought with them the knowledge of the wheel and the design of the war chariot, and were later attributed with the discovery of how to smelt iron, thus giving rise to the 'Iron Age'.

Descriptions have come down to us from the pen of a Greek writer, Poseidonius. He says:

> The Celts are terrifying in appearance, with deep-sounding and very harsh voices . . . they wear a striking kind of clothing – tunics dyed and stained in various colours, and trousers, which they call *bracae* and they wear striped cloaks . . . picked out with a variegated small check pattern. Their armour includes man-sized shields, decorated in individual fashion . . . on their heads they wear bronze helmets. . . . To the frankness and high-spiritedness of their temperament must be added the traits of childish boastfulness and love of decoration. They wear ornaments of gold, torcs on their necks, and bracelets on their arms and wrists, while people of high rank wear dyed garments besprinkled with gold.[102]

The Celts seem to have originated from an area around the Caspian Sea. Their eruption into the west came at much the same time as a similar migration into India and Persia. It is thought that the Celts and the Hindus shared a common ancestry in a race known as the Battle-Axe People, whose mark was a perforated stone battle-axe and whose home was in southern Russia; the language spoken by the Celts came from the same source as Sanskrit, the classical language of the Hindus. Thus the Celtic language is called Indo-European and it is not too far-fetched to see correspondences between the Indian deities and those of the Celts; and likenesses between the brahmins, the priest-astrologers of India, and the druids, the priest-astronomers of Europe – in fact, much has been written about the links between the two races. It is noticeable, for instance, that Celtic gods are depicted seated in a similar meditation posture to the Hindu deities, and that giant figures are carved on the hillsides of India as well as of Europe. It might even be that the woad which was painted on the bodies of Britons facing the Romans signified their allegiance to a particular god or goddess, just as the white paint on a Hindu forehead indicates a follower of Vishnu.

Physically and emotionally, however, the two peoples drifted far apart. The Hindus intermarried with older Indian races and developed a dark skin and eyes, while the Celts became renowned for their fair, reddish hair and piercing blue eyes. They were formidable warriors and were known for their boasting and threats and also for their self-dramatisation. But with great rapidity their moods would change to a dreamy sadness. Plato thought them highly intelligent, although much given to drinking.

They divided society into three groups. The druids, who were learned priests, shamans and judges; the military aristocracy, who were the power-holders and the heroes; and the free men, who were farmers and owned cattle. Both men and women were thought to be immensely brave in battle. Diodorus Siculus wrote that the Celtic women were not only like their men in their great stature (the Celts were exceptionally tall and well-built), but that they were also their equals in courage.[54] Women were honoured in Celtic society and lived in an equal way with men. A strict legal code ensured that women could inherit property, and name and title were taken from the mother rather than the father. They could marry whom they pleased and could claim damages if molested. They took their place in battle beside the men.

There were two major waves of Celtic immigration and by 700–500 BCE they had emerged as one of the most important peoples of Europe. By 387 BCE they had conquered Rome (it fell, according to the Roman historian Livy, because of the terror inspired by the 'magic' war-cry of the Celts, who went into battle naked) and by 279 BCE Delphi had fallen too, although both it and Rome were retaken later. France (known as Gaul) was entirely Celtic and Britain too became one of the Celtic strongholds as Rome advanced through Gaul. England was a centre for culture and education and the sons of Gaulish chiefs were sent there for instruction by the druids, the priests of the Celts.

Celtic culture was what the historian Nora Chadwick calls 'the fine flower of the Iron Age, the last phase of European material and intellectual development before the Mediterranean world spread northwards over the Continent and linked it to the world of today'.[41] It was also perhaps the last great mystical culture and religion of Europe, with roots going back to a prehistoric love of earth and water, trees and stars, and worship of the cosmic Mother. It was a religion of myth and legend, told and retold, forbidden to be written down. Caesar noted, 'The druids believe that their religion forbids them to commit their teachings to writing . . . because they did not want their doctrine to become public property and in order to prevent their pupils relying on the written word and neglecting to train their memories.'[32] Even in this century the tradition still exists in the remote Celtic Scottish islands. Dr Kenneth MacLeod relates that

> 'one evening a venerable Islesman, carried out of himself for the time being, allowed Dr Carmichael to take down from him a singularly beautiful 'going into sleep' rune; early next morning, the reciter travelled twenty-six miles to exact a pledge that his 'little prayer' should never be allowed to appear in print. 'Think ye,' said the old man, 'if I slept a wink last night for thinking of what I had given away. Proud indeed shall I be if it give pleasure to yourself, but I should not like cold eyes to read it in a book.'[38]

It is often taught that the Romans brought civilisation to the west, but in fact the civilisation was already there and all they did was adapt it to their own needs. Rome took from the Greeks and took from the Gauls. It is through the comments of the Romans themselves – Julius Caesar and Tacitus, for example – comments which were often used against the Celts, that we can set the record straight and appreciate the Celtic Europeans as they were before the Latin hand fell so heavily on their shoulder.

That they had a great sense of poetry and spoken literature is evident. The Greek writer, Strabo, says, 'The poets are bards, that is sacred cantors',[115] and Diodorus Siculus says, 'They express themselves in riddles . . . Friends and enemies obey the chants of the bards. Often when two armies are drawn up for battle . . . the bards launch themselves into the thick of the fighting and calm the soldiers.'[54] They were reputed to tell magical legends and were regarded by the Romans as a supernaturally gifted people.

Apart from the many accounts of the Celts by Roman and Greek historians, other sources of knowledge about them come from early Irish, Scottish and Welsh literature, which is considered to have recorded the legends and spiritual beliefs in an accurate and conservative manner. The lengthy reciting of ballads by Celtic bards is very similar to the way in which knowledge of the Indian Vedas was communicated – by scrupulously exact repetition from generation to generation. When the beliefs of the Celts were at last written down, there was considerable Christian pressure to minimise and disguise them. But Ireland in particular was a refuge for the Celts, and it remained a relatively untouched backwater, a country, even more than Wales, where the druids retreating from the Roman persecution in the first century AD could escape to, and where Roman Christianity did not settle for many centuries. There is no doubt that Irish and Welsh literature contains many accounts of pre-Roman, early Celtic beliefs.

THE SMITH AND THE FORGE

With the arrival of the Celts, the old devotion to stone began to be replaced by a mystical feeling for metal, particularly iron. Sparse meteoric deposits of iron had been in use for a long time. But when the discovery was made of how to smelt magnetite and hematite, the religious aspect of iron came to the fore.

For then, as Eliade points out, as well as the meteorites which came from the sacred vastness of the sky, there were to be found the deposits of ores deep within the womb of the Earth Mother herself.

> Metals 'grow' in the bosom of the earth. Caves and mines are assimilated to the womb of Mother Earth. The ores extracted from mines are in some sort 'embryos'. They grow slowly, as if they obey a different temporal rhythm from the live vegetable and animal organisms; nevertheless they grow, they 'ripen' in the telluric darkness. Hence their extraction from the bosom of Mother Earth is an operation performed prematurely. If they had been given the time to develop (that is, in the *geological rhythm* of time), ores would have become ripe, 'perfect' metals.[58]

Even as recently as this century, miners practised rituals and gave offerings to sacred presences which were felt to live within the mine. In the Dartmoor lead mines, the miners would leave something for Lug, a Celtic god, as well as putting part of their daily food aside for the 'knockers', spirits which could lure them into digging a faulty seam. The mine was felt to be a deep and sacred place and potentially benign or dangerous. The miner had entered an underground world, a mysterious place which he was bound by the nature of his work to violate. By his penetration into an area which was not rightfully his own, he was delivering himself up to the dark side of the Mother herself, and the Mother held the powers of life and death. Eliade makes the point that

> all the mythologies of mines and mountains, the countless fairies, genii, elves, phantoms, and spirits, are the multiple epiphanies of the *sacred presence* that the individual confronts when he penetrates into the geological levels of life.
>
> Laden with this dark sacrality, the ores are taken to the furnaces. Then begins the most difficult and the riskiest operation. The artisan takes the place of the Mother earth in order to hasten and perfect the 'growth' of the ores. The furnaces are in some sort a new, artificial womb, in which the ore completes its gestation. Hence the countless precautions, taboos, and rituals that accompany smelting.[58]

The fire is the magical means by which the ore passes from one state into another. The smelter and the smith were the masters of this process and in the old world were regarded as equal to shamans. The smith, in particular, was allotted the very power of the metal itself – the power to create objects of use and culture, and the power to destroy with weapons of war – and he was regarded with respect and fear. The sword drawn from the stone in the Arthurian legends 'suggests the sense of magic inspired by their art of producing iron from its own ore'.[34]

The divine smith, such as the Anglo-Saxon god Weyland the Smith, was to become prominent in the hierarchy of deities. It was the smith who forged the weapons of the gods. He was also endowed with healing and magical powers, and with poetry and ballad. Because his furnace replaced the earth-womb it was thus the symbol of the new mastery of time.

THE BATTLE OF THE TREES

This striking legend contains all the ingredients to make vivid the scintillating imagination of the Celts. Robert Graves has connected the battle to a real one which was fought over the occupancy of Stonehenge in about 400 BCE; but the true battle, like that portrayed in the Bhagavad Gita, was in the minds of the participants.

The sacred wood was always of primary importance to the Celts and the individual trees contained a mystical meaning. In the Battle of the Trees, the warriors themselves were transformed into trees. The account of it is given by Taliesin, a Welsh hero, and he begins it by relating the line-up of the warrior trees:

> When the trees were enchanted,
> There was hope for the trees . . .
> The alder trees in the first line,
> They made the commencement.
> Willow and quicken-tree,
> They were slow in their array. . . .[110]

Robert Graves has sifted the true battle from a number of interlinked ballads, and points out that 'the battle . . . is not a frivolous battle, or a battle physically fought, but a battle fought intellectually in the heads and with the tongues of the learned.' He notes that in all Celtic languages *trees* means *letters* and that 'the Druidic colleges were founded in woods or groves; that a great part of the Druidic mysteries was concerned with twigs of different sorts; and that the most ancient Irish alphabet, the Beth-Luis-Nion ("Birch-Rowan-Ash") takes its name from the first three of a series of trees whose initials form the sequence of its letters'.

This whole battle becomes clearer when we remember that the druids considered writing to be a form of rigidity which would detract from the spirit and forbade their teachings to be written down. 'The battle' may be about the climb-down from the spoken to the written word.

So far, so good – perhaps. But attending the battle was 'a man who could not be saluted unless his name were known', and on the other side was a woman called Achren (trees) 'whose army could not be saluted unless her name were known'.

To the warrior whose name was not known (a reference perhaps to the transcendent whose presence is not known by the spirit until it is acknowledged), the magician Gwydion, who had guessed the name, cried out, 'The high branches of the alder-tree are on your shield. Your name is Bran, of the dazzling branches. . . . The high branches of the alder-tree are in your hand; Bran you are by the branches you bear. . . . Bran, the good god, has prevailed.'[74] Thus a god, or God, was the unknown.

The god-hero, Bran, is thus represented by the alder (the woman has never been interpreted) and the magic of Bran's name is what brings him into the consciousness of the beholder. A god's name has always been sacred and very precious in all religions, especially in Hinduism, where the names of God are repeated as an enlightenment mantra. The importance attached to naming is another link between the Celts and the Hindus. But as J. Markale, a Celtic authority, points out, the real meaning of this strange battle is hidden from common eyes and can be taken at almost any level of understanding. The Celts made use of an extraordinary variety of symbols, all of which could mean several things at the same time.

> In fact, *Gwern* could mean either alder-tree, mast or marsh according to context. Having identified Bran as the alder-tree, we can use this principle of analogy to make him mast and marsh also. Indeed he is linked with both these ideas in the mabinogi of *Branwen*,[110] first as the mast of a boat when he transports his army to Ireland, and second as a marsh when he wades over the sea, less deep in those days according to Branwen. The name Bran itself (together with its variants Bron and Bren) has three different meanings: raven or crow, womb and height. He is a raven because he is a black god, the hero of the Otherworld. He is the womb because he owned the cauldron of abundance and rebirth. He is height because he was too tall to stand either in a house or a ship and was described in *Branwen* as 'the mountain that was seen alongside the ships'.
>
> Once we have understood this process of analogy, the whole of Celtic mythology opens out in a new way before our eyes. For the identification of Bran with the alder-tree is only one link in an age-old chain of interwoven ideas. Suppose

> that we start our chain with the Bran-raven equation. . . . the concept of raven can also be represented by Lug, the Celtic Mercury or Apollo. But apart from raven, Lug could also mean light (from the same Indo-European root as the Latin *lux*) and whiteness (like the Greek *leukos*). So raven gives us a whole series of analogous concepts, which runs raven-alder-mast-marsh-womb-height-light-whiteness. The raven is whiteness, the marsh is height. These startling leaps inherent in the Celts' extraordinary way of thinking are equally important in the study of present day poetical expression.[115]

It was in this way that the feeling for correspondences – for one thing corresponding to another – expressed itself in Celtic religion; an intuition which was with humanity from shamanic days. The whole world was interlinked and interrelated, a concept which is at the root of Buddhist thought too. In Celtic terms, it took its form as shifting, or metamorphosis. Heroes underwent transformations from swineherds to crows to sea-monsters to Irish kings. The wizard gods shift their shape, are invisible at will, and manifest under different forms.

It may be asked what relationship, if any, does this magical process have to real religion? A true relationship exists. The Celts had inherited from the Stone Age a sense of identity with all life in both its material and transcendent nature. They, like the cave-dwellers and the megalith-builders, saw the continual dance of the two together – the transcendent within the form and the form expressing the transcendent. The material form was never rigid and autonomous, as we see it today – never merely a 'thing', or self-created – but always liquid, dancing, filled with the otherness of the spirit. One thing could change into another because nothing was final or completed – all things had infinite potentiality.

Thus easy passage between a human hero and his archetype in the Otherworld was common in all Celtic stories: 'This is the key to the Celtic Mysteries – the merging of the spiritual, physical and imaginative planes. The later Christian insistence on a duality between light and darkness, between body and soul, between this reality and other numerous possibilities in time and space, was unknown to the Celts.'[148]

THE OTHERWORLD

In Celtic legend, one of the first occupying invasions of Ireland was by the Tuatha De Danaan, the Children of the Goddess Danu. When the Tuatha were vanquished by the Mil people, the splendid Tuatha were transformed into the gods and goddesses of the Celts. Some of them went to dwell in the megaliths and burial mounds (the 'hollow hills') which came to be called the *sidh* (the Sanskrit word for occult powers is *siddhi*). Others dived to a country beneath the sea, the 'Land under the Waves'. Most of them voyaged on into the west to Tir nan Og, the 'Land of Youth', which, with Mag Mell, the 'Land of Promise', formed the Isles of the Blest.

Both the *sidh* and Tir nan Og seem to have captured all the human yearning for a perfect place and a golden age. Time ceased to exist and a minute there could equal several years in the world. Companions of Bran, who came home after a sojourn in the Otherworld, turned to ashes when they set foot on land, for although they thought they had only been away a year in reality it was centuries.

The Otherworld was a place of supreme happiness where the land was beautiful with groves and streams, and food was abundant. No war could take place for no unsatisfactoriness existed, either in nature or in man. All people were immortal and life was spent in music and painting, poetry and love-making, chariot-racing and games. Ordinary people could only reach the Otherworld by invitation – the summons coming from a girl whose arrival was signalled by singularly sweet music, and who carried a magic apple-branch.

> Pain and treachery are unknown,
> so, too, are grief, mourning and death,
> disease and infirmity. . . .
> What a marvellous land is this!
> the young do not grow old at all.[121]

In spiritual terms, such paradise islands can be seen as places which are unchanging in a sea of change, centres of 'being' within the flux of becoming. The invitation to them is the first intimation of enlightenment and the journey demands courage, the valour of the warrior-hero. For the voyage is between the apprehension of one form of consciousness and another, and it involves the dying of the old self and the birth of a new.

For the Celts, on this journey all should be accepted and nothing taken – a profound spiritual concept which we have lost today. Whatever was offered – food, hospitality, love, directions for the next stage – should be used as the appropriate teaching of the moment, and thus the ego was surmounted. For in its strange, magical, archetypal, spiritual way, that which is given to us is always correct for the time in which we receive it. If we can learn to see what is given without struggling to over-reach ourselves in greed, we arrive at the true destination. In Celtic belief, to take what was not given meant making a choice – and whenever a choice is made, it is the ego which makes it. So 'taking' often resulted in death and obliteration. Enlightenment cannot be grasped, but it can be received.

An essential aspect of the Otherworld was the subtle, nebulous area of the intermingling of two worlds – dawn or twilight, the river's edge, the horizon, sea-mist, a bridge across a river, the rainbow, which was a sky-bridge, and birth or dying. The merging boundaries between contrasting periods of time – for instance, noon or midnight – were felt to be haunted by unseen powers. For the conception of time as divided into patterns such as the four quarters of the day, the phases of the moon, the four seasons of the year, possessed a meaning which transcended the divisions. And the divisions themselves were moments in which time was transcended and the unseen world believed to be very close.[148]

Boundaries exerted an enormous fascination on the Celts. Just like the boundaries in time, material ones on earth were in some way supernatural too, so that the line of a wood or field had a meaning beyond the everyday. A flowing river, where it crossed the boundary between parishes, was often thought to have healing powers. Unbaptised children used to be buried under boundary fences, which seems to suggest that they, like the boundary, were somehow not of this world.

To express these themes in visual ways such images were used as a sea of glass or a crystal boat. In the *Voyage of Bran*, Manannan mac Lir, God of the Seas, who carried the treasures of the People of the Sea in a crane's-skin bag and sailed in a boat which needed neither sails nor oars, created the illusion for Bran that the sea was a flower-filled land, the waves shrubs and the fish leaping lambs, so that Bran's boat seemed to float above the trees.

> There is a wood full of fine fruit
> Under the prow of your boat,
> a wood full of flowers and fruit,
> a faultless, unwaning wood,
> where the leaves are the colour of gold. . . .[121]

To the Celts, in the same way as to the Hindus, the universe was a vast illusion, and life itself was a game which was played as though it were real although fundamentally you knew that it was not the total reality. Thus there was a naturalness 'with which men, women and the gods meet and pass in and out of the natural and the supernatural spheres. In many circumstances there does not seem to have been any barrier. At times a 'druidical' mist surrounds the hero and heralds the approach of the god; at other times he appears from across the sea and perhaps a lake; sometimes a human being enters a *sidh*, a burial mound, either as a human being or as a bird; but normally the two-way traffic between the natural and the supernatural is open. In general, however, though by no means invariably, return to the land of the mortals is difficult and sometimes impossible for mortals who have visited the abode of the dead.

> A beautiful dignity hangs over Irish mythology, an orderliness, a sense of fitness. All the gods are beautifully dressed and most are of startlingly beautiful appearance. It is only by contrast with other mythologies that we realise that the 'land of promise' contains little that is ugly. There is no sin and no punishment. There are few monsters, nothing to cause alarm, not even extremes of climate. There is no serious warfare, no lasting strife. Those who die, or who are lured away to the Land of Promise, the land of the young, leave for an idealised existence, amid beauty, perpetual youth, and goodwill. The heathen Irish erected a spirituality – a spiritual loveliness which comes close to an ideal spiritual existence.[41]

THE GODDESSES

Still most central to human belief was the persona of the Goddess.

The Celtic gods, who were thinly disguised as heroes, were part of their time and place, that of an aristocratic warrior people. But the Goddess in all her forms seems to have kept her ancient attributes and persisted both through and beyond Celtic times.

The deities of the Irish Celts are all the children of the Mother, the Goddess Danu, bestower of fruitfulness and plenty. Robert Graves makes a strong case for Danu being identified with the goddess Danae of Argos, for he believes the Tuatha de Danaans to have been Bronze Age Pelasgians, expelled from Greece. But we have seen into the fallacy of the old belief that all civilisations came from Greece. Danu was also known in Britain and Gaul as Anu or Ana – a name which developed into Ann or Anne. The two mountains in Kerry, the Paps of Anu, are her breasts named after her and her fertility. He who wanted to become king of Ireland could only do so by marrying a woman who bore her name – in other words, by mating with the Earth Goddess. She was also Aine of Knochaine, 'a Munster Moon-goddess who had charge of crops and cattle and is connected in legend with the meadowsweet to which she gave its scent, and with the midsummer fire-festival'.[74]

But Anu had another side to her and could be a destroyer. Graves says she was leader of the Fate Trinity, a three-in-one triad which comprised Anu, Badb and Macha. Together they were known as the Morrigan, or Great Queen, who fought against the hero Cu Chulainn by means of constant shape-shifting. The Morrigan was maiden, bride and crone as occasion demanded, and presided over birth and death. In her moon aspect her work was at night, when she was associated with cat, snake and wolf.

Macha is believed to have been an even earlier version of the Great Goddess for she was the wife of Nemed, the leader of one of the earliest invasions into Ireland before the Tuatha. In Ulster legend she was forced to race against the horses of Conchobor while she was pregnant, and although she won the race she died giving birth to twins. While dying she put a curse on the warriors of Ulster that they should suffer for nine generations the pangs of childbirth when in their greatest need.

She was also endowed with the role of Epona, the Mare-goddess, who is depicted on many Romano-Celtic altars seated on a mare. The Celts had a love of horses and the Mare-goddess appears to have been of great significance. They decorated their horses and braided their manes, while those with richer owners wore caps. From coins of the time it appears that Celtic horsemen were so much at home on their animals that they could guide them without reins. It is believed that the prancing White Horse of Uffington is Epona's mare, cut out of the turf on the hillside before the start of the first millennium. Over 360 feet long, the great neck, back and tail flow in one long white-chalk line. The Horse bears a strong resemblance to those depicted on late Iron Age coins, thus showing its general worship. It is also probable that at Uffington Epona was actually equated with her mare and that the mare itself is her. Epona was the only Celtic goddess to be honoured at Rome.

Coventina was the Goddess of the Waters, and her sacred spring still rises outside the earth-fort on Hadrian's Wall. Her shrine contained a deep basin into which had been thrown over 14,000 Iron Age and Roman coins as well as glass, pottery and bronze figures. Water was the focal point of the Celtic spiritual life. Christianity ousted many of the 'pagan' cults of Europe, but the worship of water continued. 'The sacred wells became "holy" wells, and the goddesses who had presided over them became nymphs and guardians of wells, or saints to whom the wells were dedicated. The ghosts of white ladies traditionally associated with some wells and pools may also be dim memories of pagan goddesses.' Some 'have survived against all odds, hidden away in the depths of the countryside and still able to evoke feelings of veneration for the Earth Mother, as symbolised by a mysterious pool of life-giving water'.[23]

Water was above all an Otherworld element, fluid, mysterious, clear and unclear, both master and servant, for no man could hold it back yet it lapped at men's feet. All feminine qualities were to be found in the flow of water and the Celts worshipped it as a source of fertility, both material and spiritual, to such an extent that they dropped their greatest treasures into river, lake and stream as homage. A vast haul of golden Celtic treasure was found in the Thames; and other rivers, such as the Seine and the Severn, and lakes in Ireland and Wales, have disclosed golden torcs and coins. A haul of 190 pieces of woodcarving, including twenty complete statues, was pulled out of the Seine. These offerings were made to the mystery of life itself, as it was revealed in the flowing tides and still depths of sea, lake and river.

THE GODS

The great God of all, Dis, is rarely referred to in Celtic literature and we know of his existence mainly through Caesar:

> The Gauls affirm that they are all descended from a common father, Dis, and say that this is the tradition of the druids. For that reason they determine all periods of time by the number, not of days, but of nights [because Dis is the lord of the underworld], and in their observance of birthdays and the beginnings of months and years day follows night.[32]

Even today we follow this custom with the 'fortnight'.

Apart from Dis, it seems that many local and tribal gods existed – probably as many as four hundred – scattered throughout Celtic Europe. One reason for this is the structure of Celtic society. The *rig* (Sanskrit *raja*) was the king or chief of the tribe, which was called a *fine*. But the *fine* only contained four generations after which it split up, with one group perhaps migrating some distance away – for instance, the Parisii, who gave their name to Paris, also settled in Yorkshire. Each *fine*, or linked set of *fines*, had its own tribal deity and thus there were few national or international ones.

On the whole, there were considerably more goddesses than gods, but outstanding among those gods who were international is Lug 'of the long arm', who was widely worshipped all over Europe. Legend relates that when he went to join the Tuatha, he was asked by the guardian of the gate at Tara to declare his abilities. He said he was a carpenter, but was told that the Tuatha already had a carpenter. He was also a smith, he replied, but the Tuatha already had a smith. Having run through all his other abilities as warrior, harpist, poet, hero, historian and sorcerer and discovering that each was already present, he asked if there was any one person who was master of all these arts. Nobody could claim to be such a master and so Lug joined the Tuatha.

At once he rose to leadership for he could use both spear and sling, specialised weapons more accurate than the club. His spear was said to be a magic one which thirsted for blood and roared aloud in a fight, or flashed fire. It was he who introduced the horse in battle. He is often called the Sun-god and became a radiant

Apollo figure in Celtic religion, giving his name to towns such as Leyden, Lyons, and Carlisle. Graves tells us that when Lug sped from the west to aid the Tuatha who were in danger at the Battle of Moytorn 'Balor, the one-eyed King of the Fomori, cried out, "I wonder that the sun has risen in the west today rather than in the east." His priests answered, "Would that it were no more than the sun! It is the glowing face of Lug the Long-handed" – which nobody could gaze upon without being dazzled.' Lug won the battle against them and saved the Tuatha by sending a slingshot into Balor's one enormous eye.[74]

Lug's death on the first Sunday in August was called *Lug nasadh* – the commemoration of Lug – which wsas later changed to Lug-mass and again to Lammas. It was still observed in Ireland until quite recently with 'Good Friday-like mourning'.[74] It was kept as a feast-day in memory of the dead and the processions were led by a young man carrying a hooped wreath.

Lug, who shone like the sun, was the dispeller of darkness and despair. When the warrior hero Cu Chulainn, was exhausted and bleeding badly after single-handedly vanquishing hordes of the enemy, Lug appeared to him in all his radiance, calmly walking through the carnage of the battle. 'Who are you?' asked Cu Chulainn. 'Your father am I, from the Outerworld – I am Lug, son of Ethliu. Sleep, Cu Chulainn and I will defend you.' Examining all Cu Chulainn's wounds, he cleansed them with his gaze. Then he sang the 'men's low strain' so that Cu Chulainn fell asleep.[148]

It is thought that Caesar, who spent ten years in Gaul, equated Lug with the brilliant Roman god Mercury, for, 'Among the gods they worship Mercury. There are numerous images of him: they declare him the inventor of all arts, the guide of any road and journey, and they deem him to have the greatest influence for all money-making and traffic. After him they set Apollo, Mars, Jupiter and Minerva.'[32] Common agreement interprets Caesar as meaning Lug when he mentions Mercury, although Apollo could also be indicated. But a more likely candidate for Apollo was the Gallic Belenos, the Shining One, God of the Sun. The Celtic festival of Beltaine (meaning 'the fires of Beli') came at the beginning of May, when the cattle could be let out to pasture in the new grass. We celebrate the first of May to this day. Belenos was invoked over a large area of Europe, from northern Italy to the Shetlands. Whereas Lug was one of the Irish Tuatha, Belenos seems to have arisen from a more eastern source, possibly from Egypt.

Preceding Lug in time but of somewhat lesser importance in Ireland was the Dagda, father of the gods. The Dagda owned a club which was so heavy it had to be carried on wheels and it was said to be able to kill nine men at once. He also had a harp which played by itself. It could play three airs – the 'sleep strain', the 'laughter strain' and the 'grief strain'. His other distinctive feature was a cauldron of a size to satisfy everyone. The bronze cauldron was a prominent artefact in the late Bronze Age.

The Dagda's vast cauldron was an object of mirth to his enemies. At the battle of Fomori, a tremendous mass of porridge was put into this cauldron and the Dagda was threatened with death if he did not eat it up. But he swallowed it without trouble and even scraped the bowl.

The Dagda was a homely god, coarse in appearance, but engendering great affection. It is thought that he was the echo of an earlier cult-figure and that the arrival of the more sophisticated Lug probably displaced him. But there was never any suggestion of a quarrel between the two – rather, the Dagda gave way with fatherly affection and grace. Nora Chadwick believes that the hillside Cerne Abbas Giant, with his erect fertility phallus and great swinging club, is a representation of the Dagda.[41]

Eliade points out that the Dagda may well have been the 'Jupiter' mentioned by Caesar. Gigantic 'Jupiter figures' are found in large numbers in the countryside of France and Germany and seem to symbolise a supreme celestial god. Representations of a wheel are often found engraved on them and the wheel of four spokes was the Celtic symbol for the year – the two words 'wheel' and 'year' are identical in Celtic languages.[58] The conclusion seems to be that 'Jupiter' is the Creator of the Cosmos and the Lord of Time and that in France he was the great Dagda, father of all, although he played a more homely and comic role in Ireland.

As for the other gods mentioned by Caesar, a lot of research has failed as yet to discover their true Celtic identities. One, however, remains totally Celtic, although considerable mystery surrounds him still. He is Cernunnos (a Roman name), the horned god, and he will be discussed in the next chapter.

THE RUNNING STREAM AND THE GREEN WOOD

Perhaps the most imaginative aspect of the Celtic character was its passion for natural scenery and for the 'essence' of a particular place. The Celts seemed to be conscious in a more vivid way than we are today of how, for instance, a running stream and an ancient tree on its bank could form a sacred focus; such sanctuaries as holy springs and healing rock grottoes were popular and abundant. In general, these were in the care of the Great Mother, who would appear as a guardian spirit. Such a spirit would care for the shrine with daily ritual, manifesting as perhaps a bird or fish, a beautiful young girl or an ancient crone, according to the whim of the Mother. Even today in the remoter parts of Ireland, visions are seen of the Holy Mother by well or spring, but now her name is Mary.

Enchantment lay for the Celts in the deep intense green of woodland and field, in soft beautiful landscape – which still, in Wales or Ireland, can be felt to be secret as though, were one to walk far into the shining green woods, a magic would steal over one, changing one eternally. And still today can be found that particular silvery light – when the sky seems to be painted with silver – which belongs to the west where lay the Isles of the Blest, so beloved of the Celts.

When the Romans reached Gaul they noticed that the Celts had little use for formal buildings as places of worship, but preferred a shrine in a natural setting, usually in a grove of trees. Occasionally 'temples' have been found, such as the wooden building dating from the third century BCE on the site of London Airport at Heathrow. And in southern Germany a number of square-ditched enclosures have been excavated and found to contain burials and wooden images, implying their nature as temples. It is also likely that the megaliths such as Stonehenge were kept in use. But by and large, the Celts seem to have found the natural formations of rock and water, tree and fern, to be the sanctuaries they were most at home in. Even the Romans could share this feeling. In one of Seneca's letters, he says:

> When you find yourself within a grove of exceptionally tall, old trees, whose interlocking boughs mysteriously shut out

> the view of the sky, the great height of the forest and the secrecy of the place together with a sense of awe before the dense impenetrable shades will awaken in you the belief in a god. And when a grotto has been hewn into the hollowed rock of a mountain, not by human hands but by the powers of nature, and to great depth, it pervades your soul with an awesome sense of the religious.[34]

A real need for worship to take place in natural surroundings has continued down the centuries, so that a modern religious philosopher such as Alan Watts can say:

> When I leave the church and the city behind and go out under the sky, when I am with the birds, for all their voraciousness, with the clouds, for all their thunders, and with the oceans, for all their tempest and submerged monsters – I cannot feel Christianly because I am in a world which grows from within. I am simply incapable of feeling its life as coming from above, from beyond the stars, even recognising this to be a figure of speech. More exactly, I cannot feel its life comes from Another, from one who is qualitatively and spiritually external to all that lives and grows. On the contrary, I feel this whole world to be moved from the inside, and from an inside so deep it is my inside as well, more truly I than my surface consciousness.[165]

The Chinese had a similar feeling for landscape to the Celts, and they actually had a word for it – for the heightened dimension of being which seems to reside in one particular site. Their word was *li*, which means the innermost reality of an object, place or occasion. It is shown perfectly in the tranquility of a small fishing boat on the lake, or mist around a mountain, subjects which appealed to Celtic poet and Chinese painter alike. It was the work of the painter to identify himself with the *li* (or 'suchness') of what he painted in such a way that the painting revealed the full reality of the subject. Most people only see a surface reality; but if you were to express *li* it was necessary to drop the barrier of self and opinions and to enter completely into the rock or tree or waves that you were painting.[12]

The Celts were masters of words, and it is through their early poetry that we catch the *li* of their beloved natural world. For instance, a poem to the rowan tree expresses just that tenderness:

> You are the lovely red rowan that calms the wrath and anger of all men, like a wave of the sea from flood to ebb, like a wave of the sea from ebb to flood. . . . [94]

A stream in the valley of Traig Dha Bhan inspired this happy poem:

> Your trout out from your banks, your wild swine in your wilderness; the stags of your fine hunting crag, your dappled red-breasted fawns.
>
> Your nuts in the crest of your trees, your fish in the waters of your stream; lovely is the colour of your sprigs of arum lily, green brook in the wooded hollow. . . . [94]

With an urge to marvel, in this lyrical poem we are asked to:

> Look before you to the north-east at the glorious sea, home of creatures, dwelling of seals; wanton and splendid, it has taken on the flood-tide.[94]

Celtic poetry, the earliest poetry of western Europe, is omitted from the history books as a rule. Yet through its language we can feel our way back to a world which may seem to many of us like home.

CHAPTER SEVEN

The druids: the shaman-priests of the Celts

Much information about the druids comes to us from the Greeks and Romans. They were deeply impressed, both favourably and unfavourably, by a strange and dramatic priesthood. Their very name, dru-wid-es, means 'the far-seeing ones', a term which could mean prophetic visions, wise insight, or the more ancient shamanic vision while in flight. There is a story of Mac Roth, a druid who was sent by King Ailill to spy out where the armies of Ulster were gathering. From his report, it seems that he flew above them and observed their movements over a great area of land.[147]

For a more conventional account of their duties, however, we turn to Caesar and the reports he made for his compatriots:

> The druids officiate at the worship of gods, regulate public and private sacrifices, and give rulings on all religious questions. Large numbers of young men flock to them for instruction, and they are held in great honour by the people. They act as judges in practically all disputes, whether between tribes or individuals; when any crime is committed, or a murder takes place, or a dispute arises about an inheritance or a boundary, it is they who adjudicate the matter and appoint the compensation. . . . The druidic doctrine is believed to have been found existing in Britain and thence imported into Gaul; even today those who want to make a profound study of it generally go to Britain for the purpose. The druids are exempt from military service and do not pay taxes like other citizens. These important privileges are naturally attractive: many present themselves of their own accord to become students of druidism, and others are sent by their parents and relatives. It is said that these pupils have to memorise a great number of verses – so many, that some spend twenty years at their studies. . . . A lesson they take particular pains to inculcate is that the soul does not perish,

> but after death passes from one body to another; they think that this is the best incentive to bravery, because it teaches men to disregard the terrors of death. They also hold long discussion about the heavenly bodies and their movements, the size of the universe and of the earth, the physical constitution of the world, and the power and properties of the gods; and they instruct the young men in all these subjects.[32]

The Greek Diodorus considered them philosophers, concerned with religious affairs; and Pliny writes of them as 'diviners and physicians' – part of a general class which he termed 'magicians'.

> The druids were well versed in all learning and had the gift of prophecy; they were masters of spells and magic and could produce enchanted mists, transformations of appearance and so on whenever required. They could also impose the *geis*, a kind of magical taboo which was both injunction and prohibition, and could not be transgressed with incurring death or dishonour.[115]

Ward Rutherford, in his book *The Druids*[147] makes the point that they were not in any sense ordinary priests, and he believes that the person the Romans would have accepted as a priest was more likely to have been the local chieftain, who was often regarded as god-king-priest. If he is right and the druids were not mere priests, then we are left with an extraordinary tradition which lasted for several millennia of shaman-priest-magicians – a body of men (all accounts seem to agree on their maleness) who roamed freely over the land without being impeded by tribal boundaries, who were learned in science, mathematics, botany, medicine and astronomy; who were in charge of the appointing of kings (the old king was often ritually killed before the new one was chosen); carried out ritual sacrifice; taught orally a secret doctine, as well as conventional knowledge, which they forbade to be written down; and who possessed a mysterious 'power' which the Greek Laertius brackets with that of the Persian Magi, the 'Chaldeans' of Babylon and Assyria, and the 'seers' of Hinduism. As Rutherford points out, the clue is in the inclusion of the Magi – from which the word magic has descended – which must mean that all four groups were unusual magicians.

Yet the practice of magic is unlikely to have excited the Greeks unless there was a finer dimension implicit in it. Rutherford believes that there might have been a highly developed class of super-shamans (perhaps along the lines of some spiritual Hindu gurus). He cites the universality of the number seven – 'seven days of the week; seven Deadly Sins; seven planets; seven metals of alchemy; seven Pillars of Wisdom; seven seas; the seven-tiered Ziggurat of Babylon; the seven-branched candelabra of the Jewish temple . . . .'[147] In this century the sage Gurdjieff was to base many of his theories on the number seven – rays and octaves, worlds and elements, etc.[10] Seven is also the holy number of the Hindu Vedas, while the Irish god-hero Cu Chulainn had seven pupils in each eye, seven fingers on each hand and seven toes on each foot.[104] The choice of this number is without logical reason and can thus only be explained by a commonly agreed 'occult' significance which might bear some relation to astronomy – the seven stars of the Great Bear, for instance. As well, all three groups – Magi, brahmins and druids (the Chaldeans came to be known as magicians but did not share the same ancestry), were preoccupied with the Sacred Centre of the World, often portrayed as a cosmic tree, a concept already in existence 20,000 years earlier.

Rutherford also points out that the term 'magic', as then used, meant a possessor of wisdom. The Magi were known as the 'wise men' and it is this aspect of druidism which is often missing from modern accounts.[147]

When Rome conquered Gaul in the last century BCE, it was the druids and their influence that Caesar feared. He believed that if they united against him he could not succeed. Consequently he introduced repressive measures against them and they were forced to flee to outlying regions such as Brittany, Ireland and Wales where they would not be disturbed. The Celtic way of life continued in Ireland up to the sixteenth century (with a mixture of Christianity) and there is a strong likelihood that some druids kept their influence at least up to the seventh century – St Patrick is reported to have talked to one – but by the tenth century it was gone for good.

THE SHAMAN REDISCOVERED

As we have seen, the druids did not spring into existence brand-new. Not only was their heritage linked with ancient India, it was also the product of a very long human tradition extending back to the Ice Age and perhaps beyond. It was the tradition of interpenetration – of deity, man and earth seen as one – the three-in-one, which was to be a Celtic motif. The feeling for the earth penetrated by divine forces, and the intermingling expressed in every leaf and stone, was still as vivid for the Celts as for earlier people. An intense sense of oneness with animal life was also present. Anne Ross, an authority on the Celts, tells us that the famous druid Mac Roth wore 'the skin of a hornless dun-coloured bull' and 'a speckled bird headdress' and fluttering wings, with which he made a shamanic flight.[146] From this we can be certain that the practice of shamanism was still taking place and that the bull was the guardian animal with which the shaman in this case was identified.

We can remind ourselves here of the role of the shaman and what it implied. He was the one who brought knowledge of many dimensions of being. By his 'journey' or 'flight' he instilled the understanding in his followers that all things have their being in both this dimension of daily life and in others, of which they might not be fully aware. He was the living example of one who could move from one level of consciousness to another, and his authority was based on such a power.

The shaman's identity with a sacred animal is well attested to in Celtic times. He took on the nature of bull, stag, boar, hare, bird or fish in many stories, and in these guises entered the 'dream state' where the animal and god aspects of man are unified and merged in a timeless realm. For an animal as a guardian dwelt deeply in the Celtic consciousness and the hero relied on its power. It represented another dimension of himself and its help was often an expression of gratitude for the respect shown to it when it was helpless in the human world.

The close bond between man and animal was especially present at the grand enthronement rites, still practised as late as 1185 AD in Ulster, when a white mare was led up to the throne and the future king approached it on all fours, 'confessing himself a beast' and in this way uniting with the Mare-goddess.[115] She can be seen as a manifestation of the Mother in her Bride aspect, the colour white continuing to be her sign. In the ceremony, the mare was immediately killed and cut into pieces when the king reached it; and he bathed in a broth prepared from the blood and bones. He also drank the broth and ate the flesh (eating the flesh and drinking the blood of the god continues symbolically today in the Christian communion service). When he and the mare were thus totally become one, he was ratified as the new king. With this ritual the members of the tribe were themselves bonded to animal and earth through the new god-king.

The Celts also used art to portray animals as guardian spirits. In Britain the boar was a popular animal, appearing on shields (for protection) and crests, and also just as itself in small images. In Iberia large stone sculptures of boars were placed within the Celtic hillforts. Both the horse and the bull were animals which inspired strong feelings too. Because of the 'bull-dream' of the druid, a white bull was sacrificed at Tara on the election of a king. A three-horned bull statuette was found at Maiden Castle,while Gaul favoured the three-horned boar. Irish poets of early days wore shamanic cloaks of bird feathers to signify their affinity with particular birds which may have been seen as guardian spirits.

CERNUNNOS THE STAG-GOD

A Celtic silver cauldron, beautifully worked, was discovered in a peat bog in Jutland and is now in Copenhagen Museum. It is called the Gundestrup cauldron after its resting place. A cauldron was the symbol for rebirth among the Celts and was prominent in most of their legends, where immersion in the cauldron changed the person's consciousness from one level to another. The Gundestrup was decorated with finely moulded scenes and was undoubtedly a sacred receptacle. The Cimbri, a Celticised people who lived in Jutland, presented such a cauldron to Caesar, describing it as 'the most sacred cauldron of their country'. Like the Christian baptismal font of rebirth (for which the cauldron might have been the original), we know from such descriptions that it was an essential part of ritual worship.

One of the most striking figures depicted on the Gundestrup is a horned god with the Romanised name of Cernunnos, who sits in deep meditation with legs folded, back straight, and eyes closed. In one hand he holds out a torc, while another torc encircles his neck. The fact that the one in his hand seems to be held out as an offering gives the clue to the common wearing of torcs by all classes of society – 'it was the symbol of their unity with this all-important deity . . . '[147]

In his other hand Cernunnos holds a writhing serpent which has the head of a ram. The serpent too was an immemorial symbol of rebirth because of its wonderful ability to slough its skin and thus renew its youth. Beside the seated god are ranged a number of animals – a boar, a stag with identical horns to his own, two outlandish dogs – while decorative leaves indicate vegetation. Close by, a man rides a fish through the sea. All these are the stag-god's different manifestations. He is the lord of animals and of plants, and lord of the waters. The torc, which may have symbolised the sun, represents his 'higher' self. He can appear in one or a number of forms at the same time – man, snake, animal, vegetation, sun, or water of life – all are aspects of the one god who is both them and beyond them all. Because his horns are identical with the stag's, his shamanic role is beyond doubt, for the shamans always dressed in the likeness of the creature by whose means they would take flight. The stag was also a symbol of rebirth, for the horns are periodically renewed. But it has other complicated religious associations – it was held to be the mythical ancestor of the Celts; it was a fertility symbol as well as being a guide to the dead; and its death in the hunt made it one with the death of the hero.[58]

Cernunnos has been generally accepted as the prototype for the 'horned Devil' of western Christianity. His reputation lingers both in Brittany where, on 13 September each year, the people of Carnac celebrate St Cornely (Cernunnos) as the patron saint of horned animals, and in England, at the festival of the Deermen which takes place in Abbots Bromley every September, when the festival troupe wear ancient headdresses of deer antlers as they dance through the streets.

Cernunnos may have been Dis, the almighy founder-god referred to occasionally by the Romans as 'he from whom the Gauls claim descent'. Cernunnos is more mysterious than the other gods, his name does not appear often – which would accord with the secrecy of the druids. It would also be agreeable to the Romans, seeking to uproot all traces of druidism and to expunge all references to what must have seemed the very essence of the religion – the supreme horned shaman-god. But he was never fully suppressed, for it is he who recurs again and again in western folklore as the 'green man', the 'wild man', Merlin, Robin Hood of the green forest, Robin Goodfellow, and a host of other names.

POSSESSED BY THE GODS

> Nearly all the Gauls are of a lofty stature, fair and of ruddy complexion; terrible from the sternness of their eyes, very quarrelsome, and of great pride and insolence. A whole troupe of foreigners would not be able to withstand a single Gaul if he called his wife to his assistance who is usually very strong and with blue eyes; especially when, swelling her neck, gnashing her teeth and brandishing her sallow arms of enormous size, she begins to strike blows mingled with kicks, as if they were so many missiles sent from the string of a catapult. . . . [41]

says the Roman Marcellinus. And Tacitus, describing the conquest of Anglesey which was the stronghold of the druids, says:

> The enemy army was ranged alongside the shore like a forest of weapons and soldiers among which women ran ceaselessly about like furies, shrieking imprecations, with black robes and dishevelled hair and torches in their hands. All around stood druids with their hands raised to the sky, howling wild curses. At this sight our soldiers were gripped by fear.[156]

We can read priestesses for the women wearing black robes and carrying flaming torches. It was a common Celtic habit to appear to be possessed in the face of the enemy and thus to scare him away; while the position of women in the Celtic world was so strong – there were warrior queens such as Cartimandua of the Brigantes and Boudicca (Boadicea) of the Iceni – that it would be unusual not to find a tradition of priestesses who shared at least druid status, if not a higher one. In Ireland military service was expected of a woman until at least the seventh century and Celtic society always held them in great honour; poetesses (*banfile*) and druidesses (*bandrui*) were often honoured more than the men.

From the Roman descriptions of the battle scenes it appears that the druids, both men and women, were in the grip of a frenzy. Much would have been assumed as a fighting device, but some might have been a genuine experience, induced perhaps by hallucinatory plants or alcohol, or a mixture. For such stimulants were regarded 'as producing states of mind which approximate to the divine'. In Scandinavia 'drunkenness was regarded as a holy state and poetry itself was the "Precious Mead" '. Strabo tells us of a group of druidesses on an offshore island of Gaul (Mont St Michel immediately suggests itself) who were devoted to the cult of Dionysus – which included hallucinatory states and the drinking of alcohol.[147]

A true possession ritual would have taken place at night, by a fire, and would have been accompanied by rhythmical music such as drumming. There would have been dancing of a trance-like shamanic sort – the kind which can be seen to this day among the Sufis, who dance in ritual circles to awaken five centres of illumination. This procedure is said to bring about a change of consciousness and an expansion of the mind. To the druids, such an expansion – helped along by hallucinatory plants and by mead – would have led to becoming one with the deity and thus being 'possessed' by it.

We know that the druids used drums, that they met by night in sacred groves, and that they drank mead – the name of the Irish goddess-queen Medb, or Maeve, derives from the word 'mead' and she is referred to as 'the Drunk-making Woman'.[115] With such ingredients, as well as the tradition of shamanism, the 'black-robed women, shrieking like furies' can be seen as properly 'possessed' as they tried (in vain) to defend their holy island.

RITUAL SACRIFICE

Another feature of the Gundestrup cauldron is a scene in which a sacrifice seems to be going on. A man wearing a cap with a long tassel, almost certainly a druid, is putting another smaller man head first into a cauldron. This scene has long been accepted as part of the plethora of evidence that the Celts sacrificed humans as well as animals. But there could be another explanation:

> When one takes the scene on the Gundestropp Cauldron in conjunction with the legends of warriors brought back to life through immersion in a magic cauldron, one is left wondering whether this is not what is actually being portrayed here and whether the smaller figure is not really a corpse, perhaps fallen in battle, especially as the other figures on the same plate are warriors. Is this, in other words, a portrayal of regeneration through divine intervention?[147]

The very thought of ritual human sacrifice sends a shudder down the spine, which is odd when one considers the mindless and highly unsanctified slaughter going on in our society today. So perhaps we should look a little more closely at what sacrifice meant.

The word sacrifice comes from *sacrum facere*, which means to 'make sacred'. It

> was used to describe an act of self-transcending through which the individual sought to attain the divine. It has now come to denote very little more than the killing of an animal or a man as an offering to the divinity either by way of supplication or thanksgiving; and Christianity has further devalued the word by associating it with notions of austerity and self-denial.[115]

But to identify sacrifice with mortification is a serious error

> since it totally alters the nature of the spiritual process by which the Ancients sought to fulfil their destiny. Ritual sacrifice was never intended to deprive creation for the sake of the creation. . . . Sacrifice was first and foremost a psychic procedure in which the sacrificial 'victim' threw off the burden of earthly dross and rose through a series of stages in his attempt to reach the divinity. This divinity might be the Perfect being, the Great Mother, or an objective god or some concept of the ideal which was inherent in the individual.[115]

That a victim could be willing and eager for his fate does not strike modern man as probable. But as we have seen, the significance of the act of sacrifice was a sublime giving up in order to receive – the victim became the god in the same way that the Communion bread and wine *are* the body and blood of Christ. The Romans noticed many instances of young men throwing themselves into the sacrificial fires and there can be no question but that this heroic act was believed to be the right way of uniting with the transcendent. And those druids and warriors who sacrificed their victims by fire or drowning would share this belief. If an animal was sacrificed as a human substitute, it too would be part of that same destiny. The simple explanation so readily given by historians that a sacrifice was to appease an angry god or win his favour fails to penetrate the subtleties of the act. 'The victim was a messenger for the community fulfilling the ritual, a messenger whose association with the divinity would make him a link between that particular god and mankind.'[115]

The Romans had given up the practice of human sacrifice shortly before they conquered the Gauls, and Caesar's references to it are tinged with a holier-than-thou colour. It is now thought that he described some scenes in an unlikely way, for it was to his political advantage to paint the druids in a bad light. His description, for instance, of the gigantic wicker figure of a man which was filled with living victims and then set alight (vividly portrayed in the film *The Wicker Man*) is believed to be pure imagination, since no other reference to the custom has ever been found.

Pliny, a less shakeable Roman witness than Caesar, gives the only detailed account of a druid ceremony

> This [the ceremony] was determined by observing the growth of mistletoe on an oak tree, a circumstance of rare occurrence. The time chosen for the subsequent rite was the sixth day of the moon, and preparations were made for a feast and a sacrifice of two white bulls. A Druid in a white robe climbed the tree and cut with a golden sickle . . . the branch of mistletoe, which was caught as it fell on a white cloak. The bulls were then sacrificed.[136]

The berries of the mistletoe while still growing are white, although they turn golden after picking – which might account for a golden-coloured sickle. This would accord with the shamanic aspect of the whole ceremony, for the gold would represent the sun and the white the moon. The druid's dress would be donned for the occasion (they certainly did not wear white gowns all the time, as modern pictures would have us believe).

The druidical sacred tree was the oak. Tacitus, describing the Celtic Germans, talks of 'consecrated forests and groves, calling by the name of gods that hidden power which they behold only with the eyes of reverence'.[155] Lucan describes a forest grove near Massalia, which Caesar had destroyed by hacking down the trees:

> A grove there was, untouched by men's hands from ancient times, whose interlacing boughs enclosed a space of darkness and cold shade, and banished the sunlight from above. No rural Pan dwelt there, nor Silvanus, ruler of the woods, no Nymphs; but gods were worshipped there with savage rites, the altars heaped with hideous offerings, and every tree was sprinkled with human gore. On these boughs . . . birds feared to perch; in those coverts wild beasts would not lie down; no wind ever bore down upon that wood, nor thunderbolt hurled from black clouds; the trees, even when they spread their leaves to no breeze, rustled among themselves. Water also fell there in abundance from dark springs. The images of the gods, grim and rude, were uncouth blocks, formed of fallen tree-trunks. . . .[136]

Such a passage could be used as it stands in a Gothic horror story and it is as well to remember not only that the Romans had only just stopped sacrificing people themselves but also that any justification for crushing the druids, such as a blood-smeared sacred grove, was seized upon.

There were three principle methods of sacrifice – burning, drowning and hanging or throttling. These methods accorded with the three elements of fire, water and air and were said by Lucan to have been dedicated to three gods: Taranis (burning), Teutates (drowning) and Esus (hanging). The victims who were sacrificed to Teutates had their heads held under water in a pot or cauldron, while those sacrificed to Esus were hung upside down from a tree and then stabbed. They may have been throttled as well, for a 'triple death' was not uncommon. The bog-man recently found in Cheshire and dating to the sixth century BCE had been garrotted, stabbed through the arteries and probably smothered as well. The spilt blood was poured on tree and earth and was undoubtedly thought to be a source of sacred fertilisation. To the Romans, such smearing of blood was repellant, but there is little indication that they understood its purpose.

Sacrifices were also made in battle. It was the custom for the Celts to kill all their prisoners as a tribute to the gods. Punishment for criminals was by burning. Strabo reports that a large number of criminals meant an equally large yield for the land.

Yet another form of sacrifice is described in a Connaught story. It tells of a maiden who had many wooers. At Samhain (the beginning of the Celtic year on 1 November) each suitor was found a substitute from his community who was killed in his place. 'Not much interpretative skill is required to understand that the "maiden" is a goddess and that each community of her worshippers provided one sacrificial victim.'[147]

THE CULT OF THE SEVERED HEAD

A severed head is an aspect of sacrifice which sends another frisson down the spine. The Celts believed that a person's whole soul lay within the head, and this was both the sacred and the human centre. As such it was supremely powerful – thus to leave a head lying in battle was to degrade that power. Throughout history mankind has always believed that something of the person remained after death, which is why graves are tended and special days set aside to visit the resting place of ancestors. Tibetans believe that there is a period of some days between the death of the body and the realisation of death by the psyche. It may be that the Celts also felt that the head would remain potent for some time after death, for enemy's heads were always strung around the victor's horses. Strabo tells us:

> There is also that custom, barbarous and exotic, which attends most of the northern tribes . . . when they depart from the battle they hang the heads of their enemies from the necks of their horses, and when they have brought them home, nail the spectacle to the entrance of their houses.[136]

Heads were also placed in niches or on pillars. Chadwick tells us that the sanctuary at Rocquepertuse in France, which was divided into two superimposed terraces, 'was decorated by a portico of quadruple stone pillars containing niches to hold and display human skulls . . . and on the cross beam which joined the pillars was perched a stone bird over half a metre in height, about to take flight.'[41] Here is the authentic shamanic correspondence between the head, seat of the soul, and the bird whose flight will carry the spirit to its union with the divine (druids were well known for their ability to interpret the cries of birds and were believed to understand bird language). In this amazing sanctuary we even have our old friend, the anthropomorph.

> The pillars, pierced with sockets in the shape of skulls, had been painted with geometric designs, and with living beings such as fish, flying birds and horses. . . . There are anthropomorphic statues wearing a torc and an armlet, and another with a belted tunic, also with polychrome decoration, and seated in the Buddha-like attitude.[41]

Nowhere do we have a more certain confirmation that the cult of the head was a sacred practice. We may feel repelled by it, but their wisdom was different from ours. In the Welsh Mabinogi of *Branwen*, the hero, Bendigeid Vran, was slain and his head removed by his companions who, knowing it contained a magical quality, carried it away with them. After seven years they took the head to Gwales.

> And there they remained four score years, unconscious of having ever spent a time more joyous and mirthful. And they were not more weary than when first they came, neither did they, any of them, know the time they had been there. And it was not more irksome to them having the head with them than if Bendigeid Vran had been with them himself. And because of these fourscore years it was called the entertaining of the noble head.[110]

The carving of heads out of stone was one of the basic Celtic art forms. Long-faced, they gaze at us from museum, garden or churchyard. They are sometimes crudely formed, sometimes fine, but always with a compelling power. Professor Ross has suggested that church and house gargoyles may well be survivors of this art. Heads were also made into goblets. Herodotus describes the process of sawing the skull off above the eyebrows, clearing the interior and covering the result in gold or leather. He also describes seeing them set up on staves 'so that the head sticks up far above the house, often above the chimney'. In this position the head guarded the whole house, he was told.[136]

Heads were also closely connected with water worship and many have been discovered in wells and pools. One of the best known holy wells in Britain is that of St Winifred in Wales. She was beheaded by Prince Caradoc when she refused his advances. Water gushed from the earth where her head fell and she herself was miraculously restored to life.

Rutherford reminds us that the seed-head of a plant is always found at the plant's top and that this fact must have been of the greatest importance in Neolithic farming and might well have led to a belief that the seed of man was also in his head. At the same time in history, in China, a small hole used to be bored in the top of the head to enable the spirit to shoot out in its ascent to divinity.

And indeed we ourselves believe that the head is the centre and mediator of our lives. We may quote scientific knowledge to prove our point but we need hardly do so because we *believe* it. So we should not find it too difficult to understand a people who saw the head as the source of presence, of curative strengths, and of transformative powers.

REINCARNATION

Implicit in their easy attitude to death was the Celts' belief in rebirth, a druidical teaching. The Celts held with certainty to the understanding that death was merely a slight pause in a long life and consequently they had very little fear of it, as Caesar noted. 'Souls do not die, but after death, pass from one body to another; and this belief, as the fear of death is thereby cast aside, they hold to be the greatest incentive to valour'[32]; and Lucan adds, 'the same breath still governs the limbs in a different scene'.[115]

The Celtic doctrine of reincarnation is well described by the warrior-poet Taliesin, in *The Battle of the Trees*. He himself claimed to have led many different lives as both human and animal and to have witnessed most of the major events in Irish history. He declares:

> I have been in many shapes
> Before I attained a congenial form . . .
> I have been a drop in the air
> I have been a shining star . . .

I have been a bridge for passing over
Three-score rivers,
I have journeyed as an eagle
I have been a boat on the sea. . . .[110]

The chant of Amergin, a very early poet, seems to be on the same lines but with the added depth that 'he has actually taken on the nature of other things and other creatures, and that this has made him entirely at one with the universe, peaceful in spirit and great in mind':[115]

I am the wind which blows over the sea,
I am wave of the sea,
I am lowing of the sea,
I am the bull of seven battles,
I am an eagle on the rock,
I am a tear of the sun,
I am skilful sailor,
I am a boar for courage,
I am lake in the valley,
I am word of knowledge,
I am a sharp sword threatening an army,
I am the god who gives fire to the head,
I am he who casts light between the mountains,
I am he who foretells the ages of the moon,
I am he who teaches where the sun sets.[121]

Graves points out that the commonest 'I have been' or 'I am' poems also refer to the cycle of the year, and that they contain a complete series of 'round-the-year' symbols, although confused deliberately so that the secret could not be discovered. But as it is only a deity who can be responsible for the whole cycle of the year, we can still be certain that it is the poet-god who is describing existence in his own special way.

The cosmic significance attached to the cycle of the seasons and to the boundaries of time such as day and night is captured in a story from the Book of Leinster. The Dagda, who had apportioned all the *sidh* mounds in Ireland to the Tuatha de Danaan, was approached by Mac Oc, who wanted some land. 'There is none for you,' said the Dagda, 'All the divisions have been made.' 'Then let me have a day and a night in your own dwelling,' begged

Mac Oc. This was granted. When the Dagda came back twenty-four hours later, Mac Oc was still in the *sidh*. 'Go now,' said the Dagda, 'since you have finished your time.' 'It can be seen,' replied Mac Oc, 'that night and day are the whole world; and it is that which you gave to me.' The Dagda then left and Mac Oc stayed in the *sidh*.[152]

Such subtle fluidity bewildered the logical Romans and has baffled many scholars since, for it does not accord with Latin or Semitic religious concepts. The Celts 'understood their own lives and the universe itself as being guided by a single internal movement'.[147] Thus they did not believe in the duality of good and evil, and there was no such place as hell nor any justice meted out after death. The easy merging of life and death is aptly illustrated by a story in the Welsh romance of *Peredur*, called 'The Ford of Souls' (a ford or bridge was often used as a symbol for the point of contact between the world of the living and other worlds). In the story, a flock of white sheep stood on one bank and on the other was a flock of black sheep. When a white sheep bleated, a black sheep would cross the water and turn white. When a black sheep bleated, a white sheep would cross the water and turn black. Thus the living and the dead changed their identities with simple ease.[110]

This same story reflects the Celtic feeling for inner balance. The Chinese yin and yang, also represented by black and white, are primal, active pairs, such as feminine and masculine, I and other. When they are perfectly balanced a harmonious energy called *ch'i* is produced; when they are out of balance, a force called *sha* operates, which means they have become separated or unmoving. The Celts were conscious of an innate need for *ch'i*, which is perhaps why the druids conducted all their ceremonies in the open by water, or among trees. For there is another force which perhaps we could call

> 'angelic interference' which tends to bring the out-of-balance yin and yang into equilibrium. It is this quality which, when associated with a well, for example, makes it into a holy well, for the water from a well will tend to re-balance the energies in people, making them 'whole'. . . . It is 'angelic interference' which makes an otherwise ordinary site both holy and healthy.[75]

We look in vain, however, if we try to find anything so formalised and structured as a principle or ultimate doctrine of rebirth among the volatile and swift-thinking Celts. Perhaps the nearest to a doctrinal statement was made by a Celtic hero talking to St Patrick. St Patrick asked him, 'Who or what was it that maintained you so in your life?' The answer came, 'Truth that was in our hearts, and strength in our arms, and fulfilment in our tongues.'[136] The Celts lived their beliefs and did not objectify them. Their concept of time was not ours – whether life-time or death-time. The Breton story-tellers would always begin, 'Once upon a time, there was no time, and it was then that . . .'[115] They lived by myth which 'is not the retelling of events; it is the programme of the events themselves'.[147] Their myths could be understood on any number of levels according to the capacity of the hearer – as sheer fairy story, as shape-shifting for magical ends, as visits to other worlds, or as union with the deity.

THE NUMBER THREE

The druids, Posidonius tells us, 'teach many things to the nobles of Gaul in a course of instruction lasting as long as twenty years, meeting in secret in a cave, remote woods or valleys'.[104] Caesar adds that the druids taught in triads – verses of three statements or phrases. This tradition was maintained in Ireland until the English conquest. A ninth-century Irish poem gives a fine example:

I have news for you; the stag bells, winter snows, summer has gone.
Wind high and cold, the sun low, short its course, the sea running high.
Deep red the bracken, its shape is lost; the wild goose has raised its accustomed cry.
Cold has seized the birds' wings; season of ice, this is my news.[94]

The number three was of obsessive importance to the Celts. There are three-headed goddesses and gods (although double-headed images are also found, suggesting the Celtic intuition of looking in two directions at the same time). The harvest goddesses – the Matronae – are always depicted in threes, as is the evil Morrigan.

The heroes too can appear three times in the same adventure with different names and characters, which makes for such confusion that it is a temptation to drop the story in despair. For in our down-to-earth, materialistic world, the elusive, irrational, shape-shifting magic of the Celts is out of place, and it is only when we push aside our boundaries and allow ourselves to exist in a more intangible dimension that something of their magic appears.

Perhaps the highest meaning of the three-faced gods and of the great reverence for the number three has to do with a belief also found in the kindred Hinduism. There, the three gods called Brahma, Vishnu and Shiva form a triad representing three aspects of the Supreme Reality. Brahma is the creator, Vishnu the preserver and Shiva the destroyer of the world, the last being necessary for new creation. We can find all three activities in our own lives. The whole cycle of existence as symbolised by a divine trinity is common to many ancient religions. The Celtic symbol for the three-in-one was the triskele, a two-directional spiral similar to the Chinese yin and yang but with a third spiral added, which was later called by alchemists the Secret Fire. The triskele was an archetypal symbol of great power and was depicted all over the Celtic world.

THE RIDDLE OR THE KOAN?

The riddle was another teaching device used by the druids, according to Caesar. In the last chapter we learnt of the riddle of 'the man who could not be saluted unless his name was known'. Perhaps the druids used the riddle as Zen masters used the koan, in the hope of breaking through their pupil's clinging to only one dimension of reality. Thus the poet Amergin ends a verse by asking:

> I am a wizard: who but I
> Sets the cool head aflame with fire?
> I am an infant: who but I
> Peers from the unknown dolmen arch?[121]

The child Taliesin went to rescue Elphin, imprisoned by his uncle at Dyganwy, and secured Elphin's release by confounding all the twenty-four court bards, as well as the chief bard himself. First he silenced the bards with a spell and then he recited a long riddling poem which they could not solve. The climax of the story came with a final riddle:

> Discover what it is:
> The strong creature from before the flood.
> Without flesh, without bone,
> Without vein, without blood,
> Without head, without feet . . .
> In field, in forest . . .
> Without hand, without foot . . .
> It is also as wide
> As the surface of the earth,
> And it was not born,
> Nor was it made. . . .[110]

The answer, which is 'The Wind', was made not verbally but practically with a hurricane of wind which frightened the king into bringing up Elphin from his dungeon. Taliesin then freed him from his chains with an incantation.

John Sharkey retells a delightful riddle situation: 'A queen is sitting on the grass. The Druid passes by, and she asks him what is the present hour good for? "For begetting a king on a queen," he answers. The girl saw no other male near her so she took him inside her.'[148]

To the uninitiated, such as the Romans, most of the Celtic beliefs – for instance, three gods in one – would have seemed to be on the level of riddles, and the druids would have wanted to keep it that way as much as possible.

In many ways the Celts and their druids defined our own culture and we shall meet their influence again in later chapters. They lived a warrior's life, which has been defined in our time as 'not being afraid of who you are'[10] – and, we could add, not being afraid of the world about you. Their free-flowing consciousness of other dimensions of reality, their fearlessness, and their total acceptance of death as part of life are attitudes we may envy in our more tightly inhibited world. For the separation between living and dying has now become absolute to us and we fear death in a way which would have been incomprehensible to the Celts. To them, life and death were both implicit with meaning, and it is our sad loss today that many people fail to see any meaning in their lives beyond the humdrum. Most important of all, the Celts lived on a highly *personal* level, and however barbaric and cruel their ways may seem to us they would not have understood the cold-blooded maiming and killing which takes place everywhere today.

CHAPTER EIGHT
The gods of Rome and Greece

The Romans, brilliant at administration, had little inclination to open themselves to the infinite realm of the mystery of the spirit. Their character was more suited to an established state religion, orderly, seemly and unmystical. In ways that remind one of the traditional Church of England, their religion was respectable and proper and did not demand from the individual any great commitment or spiritual upheaval. Religious practice took the form of pious duties, both to family and state, while the gods themselves were slightly enlarged extensions of the human scene, individuals who could be approached with petitions and who responded to the correct ritual. Roman religion was essentially practical and utilitarian, corresponding to the needs of an unimaginative although just people. The gods were not worshipped with awe and passion but were regarded as necessary protectors whose benefits must be paid for – a shopkeeper religion.

Perhaps because of the uninspiring nature of their worship, the Romans were amiably inclined towards the faiths of other peoples. It was not in their judicial character to object to strange beliefs unless those beliefs led to insurrection. But any threat to their supreme power, as in the case of the Jews and also the druids, and there would be no dispute about the necessity of eradicating a disruptive belief. Initially there was toleration for the Jews and Christians until it became clear that they would not accept the gods of Rome – an attitude which was incomprehensible to the Romans.

The gods themselves were by no means purely Roman, but were largely imported from Greece and the Orient. But some were indigenous. In fact there was a register of purely Roman gods, an original catalogue which listed them and gave their functions and protective powers, and also the rites which would invoke those powers. But as the Roman empire spread over the world, the gods of other peoples, even enemies, were accepted without demur by the Romans and simply added to their own pantheon as new protectors of family and of the heart of the empire, Rome itself. By the first century AD gods and goddesses from Greece, Asia Minor, Persia, Syria and Egypt, as well as some of the Celtic deities such as Belenus and Epona, had all become an integral part of Roman religion.

The Greek mystery cults in particular came to influence the Roman world. Their carefully guarded rites and initiations provided intelligent Europeans with a treasure-trove of thought, philosophy and worship at a deeper level than any practised in Rome itself. For instance, the Greek mysteries provided a brilliant understanding of the way in which music and form go together. When a building was erected which contained certain principles of architecture it was compared to a musical chord which must satisfy the mathematics of its harmonic intervals. In this way, vibration was used in the creation of special chambers where the whispering of a word in one room would be so powerfully carried that a roar would fill the whole building. Such knowledge pervaded the mystery cults at their higher levels. Both the cults and the deities which came to influence the western world are studied in this chapter.

MARS, GOD OF THE SOLDIERS

Mars is the most purely Roman of all the gods. He is usually thought of as a god of war but in more ancient rural Italian history he was the god of vegetation and fertility, living in forests and mountains. His other name was Silvanus (who later became a separate deity) and he was particularly responsible for the welfare of cattle and crops. That fundamental need of the human to be in touch with the source of fertility was expressed in the worship of Silvanus-Mars.

He was the son of the great goddess Juno, the consort of Jupiter. But his conception was not with the aid of Jupiter but by Juno's mystical union with a flower. In his turn, he took by surprise the virgin Sylvia while she was asleep, and thus became the father of the twin founders of Rome, Romulus and Remus. The she-wolf who suckled the twins is always to be seen with Mars in his Silvanus aspect, as are the woodpecker and the horse.[104]

His name, Mars, comes from the root *mar*, to shine. He was a sun deity in Etruria and Umbria and was also the god of spring, when the most important agricultural rites and festivals were celebrated. He was then known as Mars Gradivus, meaning 'to grow' and 'to become big'.

This meaning became changed to the verb *gradi*, to march, when he lost his rural forest aspects as Silvanus, was adopted by Rome, and became the warrior god of battle. Offerings were made to him before a battle began and if the battle was won he received some of the takings. In the end he became one of the foremost war gods of Rome and altars to him can be seen all over Europe, sometimes showing sacrificial scenes in which a bull, ram or pig was the victim.

Strangely enough, Celtic influence returned Mars to his first nature as a god of peace and fullness. In northern Britain he retained his war role but in southern Britain, France and Germany he was transformed into a god of healing.

MERCURY, THE TRADER GOD

Mercury was a god who appealed to the Celts and, as we have noted, he came to be identified with the Gallic god Lug. Mercury was a herald, and because he was deemed equivalent to the Greek Hermes, he became a messenger to the gods. As such he was widely worshipped and many small figurines of him have been found. Unlike Mars, whom the Celts occasionally represented in strange match stick-man form, Mercury inspired complex bronzes. On one of these bronzes, found in the Roman city of Verulamium (St Albans), Mercury wears a silver torc, a Celtic deity symbol, while a cockerel stands on his left side as the herald of a new dawn – to echo his role as herald of the gods. A tortoise is by his feet to represent his invention of a lyre from a tortoise shell. His right hand holds the phallic horn of a ram, symbolising fertility – and perhaps success in trading. According to Tacitus, he was particularly worshipped by the German tribes beyond the Rhine who, he says, 'count it no sin to win his favour on certain days by human sacrifice'.[156] Tacitus decided that the Roman deities comprising Hercules, Mercury and Mars had their counterparts in the German Thor, Woden and Tiu. Sacrifices were made to all these gods by the Germans but the figure of Woden-Mercury was the most important.

THE WISE GODDESSES: MINERVA AND ATHENE

One of the three state deities of Rome, Minerva was a goddess of the thunderbolt of wisdom. Very early in Roman history she merged her identity with the more ancient Greek goddess Athene, and became the protectress of commerce and learning. Considerably later, she took on the persona of a warrior-goddess (as did Athene) and was honoured with Mars in a spring festival, the Quinquatrus, which lasted five days. She was venerated throughout the Roman empire, particularly by doctors and musicians.

In Britain she came to be identified with the Celtic goddess of healing, Sul, and was actually Sulis Minerva. When the Romans discovered the therapeutic powers of the thermal waters at Bath, Sulis Minerva came to preside over the spring and her statue can be seen there to this day. Recent excavations at Bath have retrieved over 6,000 coins thrown into the water at her feet.[76]

In Minerva's double identity with Athene, she inherited a role as protector of the brave. She personified all that was loved in womanhood – gentle strength, succour to those in need, and the power of healing through water. And yet Athene is perhaps the most ancient known instance of the psychological subjugation of woman to man. For the myth of her birth is a deeply significant one.

Her father, Zeus, highest god of all Greece – and extremely amorous into the bargain – had taken as his first wife the goddess Metis, who was infinitely wiser than all the gods and represented the Mother Goddess herself. She was also a shape-shifter and changed her shape whenever Zeus approached her. At last, by a trick, he conquered her and she conceived. Zeus then learnt that if she had another child it would be the end of him. So, while she was pregnant, he swallowed her at a gulp. Some time later, while walking beside a lake, he began to feel an intense headache. It grew at such a rate that he howled with pain. The god Prometheus took a double axe and split his head open whereupon his daughter Athene sprang out, giving a battle shout.

Campbell sees Athene's birth as a birth from the father's brain, just as a woman gives birth from the womb.

> Creation by the power of the Word is another instance of such a transfer to the male womb: the mouth the vagina, the word the birth. And one extremely important consequence of this bizarre, but highly honoured, aberration upward, is the notion, common to all Occidental spirituality – and particularly stressed by our numerous bachelor and homosexual great teachers – that spirituality and sexuality are opposed.[34]

Such a 'birth from the brain' brings about the devaluation of the body, particularly the female body; and all patriarchal mythology has systematically denigrated and diminished the role of woman, while emphasising the power of man to give brain-birth. Such an attitude took its time to spread throughout Europe, but the birth of Athene and her continuance into Minerva perhaps marked its beginning.

The ancient bird-goddess of prehistory re-emerged in forms of Athene. She can sometimes be seen winged and a bird is her constant attribute. In Corinth a bird with a woman's head is shown perching behind her. It was believed that she appeared as an owl in a battle against the Persians, and she was often invoked as a dove or sea-bird. She is thus a strangely powerful goddess, with levels of meaning all of which, perhaps, have not yet been revealed.

JUNO AND JUPITER, THE REIGNING DEITIES

Juno was a very great Roman goddess, head of all other goddesses in the state religion and embodying the feminine principle of heavenly light, of which her brother and consort, Jupiter, was the masculine principle. She was also a moon-goddess and appeared in another of her aspects as Diana, the moon-huntress. Because she personified light, she was prayed to at childbirth, for a new born baby is brought into the light, and hence into her presence.

She was protectress of Rome itself and it was her sacred birds, the geese, which warned the Romans when the Gauls tried to climb over the city walls. As a protectress of birth and life she also in time became a liberator; one who was always available to give help and to set free those imprisoned – either in body or mind. In this sense, her moon aspect was the one to be sought, for the moon was believed to be the first stage on the journey to higher worlds. It was the realm of souls after death, who remained there until they fell back to earth into a new life. For her ability to confer protection and entry into a new world, Juno was revered and loved throughout the Roman empire.

Her consort-brother, Jupiter, was brilliance itself, god of sun and moon and of all sky phenomena – wind, rain, thunder and lightning. He was a true cosmic god, his realm the sky and his weapon the thunderbolt. His thunderbolt was also divine knowledge, which can come to a person with sudden force, while his lightning streak was enlightenment, lighting up the darkness of the mind.

Jupiter's characteristics appealed to people of the Middle East and he gradually came close to merging with the father-god of the Jewish and Christian faiths, although he never lost touch with mankind. In the Celtic west, particularly in Gaul and Germany, he became identified with a thunder-god, Taranus. In Britain he seems to have merged with a Celtic sun-god, whose symbol was the spoked wheel but whose Celtic name has never been known. Jupiter is depicted in bronze as a young, naked god with his foot placed on the head of a being who is disappearing into the earth. The god is surrounded by an eagle (the Jupiter emblem), a sun-wheel, a dolphin and a triple-horned bull's head. The wheel and the eagle are sky symbols, the bull is merging with the earth, while the dolphin almost certainly represents the seas – thus giving Jupiter power over the whole cosmos.[34]

MITHRA AND THE MYSTERIES

By the first century AD, eastern culture had penetrated the Roman world through oriental trade and merchants, and through Roman colonisation. The mystery religions of the east seem to have held great attractions for the Romans and the reasons are not hard to understand, since we see similarities in our own times.

The state religion of Rome was an incredibly dull affair, impersonal and static, demanding little of the individual beyond prescribed acts of ritual. But the cults of the east involved a deeper relationship between the person and the divine. Through actual deeds of selflessness, meditation, initiation and proper conduct, a person could attain insight into the ultimate nature of the universe; and happiness in both this and future lives. The process of secret initiation into higher realms made the whole nature of religion one charged with possibilities; and it brought a sense of real relationship between human and deity which was lacking in the uninspired rites of Roman officialdom.

Mithra, a god imported from Persia, inspired a cult which spread from Syria to Scotland. The cult first flowered in the Near East in the fourth century BCE when Mithra, a messenger of light and a hero-saviour, was sent to earth by the great Persian deity Ahura Mazda, to hunt and slay a Primeval Bull whose blood was the source of all fertility.

In the most familiar image of Mithra, one which was reproduced throughout Europe, he can be seen kneeling on the collapsed bull, his sword deep within the animal's shoulder from which flows, instead of blood, a stream of grain. A serpent, symbolising the renewal of the life-cycle, glides alongside. A dog, in Iran the mythic first friend and counterpart of man, reaches up to eat the falling grain, for he is the archetypal life-form to be nourished by this sacrifice; while a scorpion grasps the bull's testicles to show the death of the creative force – for death as much as life is part of the process of existence. It is thought by some that the face of Mithra, in the better examples of this sacrifice, shows an expression of sadness and compassion as he stabs the bull, as though he is taking to himself that guilt which has always haunted mankind – the guilt of killing in order to live.[34]

The mystery cult of Mithra in Hellenistic Greece, where it rose to its height, took place in a cave or grotto at night and included in its masked rites an actual bull sacrifice. The initiate lay in a pit below the death-stall, so that when the sword-blade entered the bull the warm spurting blood would pour over him. Two attendants on either side of the bull held flaming torches, one turned up and the other down, to represent the ascent of light to the upper world and its descent to the lower depths (these torchbearers are often equated with the good and bad thieves on either side of Christ, for torches in the same up-and-down-pointing positions were used to represent the thieves in enactments of the Crucifixion). The whole bull ceremony was a celebration of the energy of opposites – life and death, the spring and autumn equinoxes (Taurus the bull at spring and Scorpio the scorpion at autumn – for the astrological zodiac was already devised), and the encircling energy arising from the sacrifice itself, which untied the opposites and turned matter into energy. Finally the bull, as the Primeval Being, would be cut up and buried to ensure the growth of crops. Such a scene, apparently so brutal, may appal us; that is, unless we have watched the impersonal cattletrucks taking their victims to the abattoir for a ceremony unmotivated by any semblance of respect or worship.

Much of the appeal of the Mithra cult lay in its system of initiations, of which there were seven. The new initiate was called a Raven and his task was to make his way back to enlightenment by way of seven stages. It was believed that the unborn soul on its descent to earth had passed through the seven visible orbits of Moon, Mercury, Venus, Sun, Mars, Jupiter and Saturn. These orbits were conceived as envelopes surrounding the earth. In each envelope the unborn soul received a specific characteristic, which was capable of both helping and hindering him. One by one, he had to return to these orbits, redeeming the limitations on his character as he passed until, the seven stages completed, he entered into the realisation of the unconditioned state.[66]

The Raven, bird of death, with whom in shamanistic fashion the initiate was identified, carried him symbolically through the Moon orbit – which symbolised both the waxing and the waning of the life-force and the essential sustenance of vegetation. As Raven, with his body symbolically dropped, the initiate flew on to Mercury, which was the sphere of rebirth, of occult wisdom and of magic. If he passed this stage he became known as the 'Hidden Master' and proceeded on to Venus, orbit of the delusions of desire. Safely past Venus, he became the 'Soldier' who rose to the Sun, the sphere of the intellect and power of knowledge, where he was presented with a crown lying on a sword. He had to push away this material crown, announcing Mithra as his true spiritual crown. He then became a'Lion' and took part with his equals in a sacramental repast of bread and water mixed with wine, which was a sign of his graduation. Passing on through the Sun orbit he came to Mars, centre of courage and audacity (one can imagine the terrifying tests at this point). Here he was given, if successful, a special Phrygian cap and the Iranian dress of the Saviour Mithra. His last two stages of transformation were into Jupiter, Runner of the Sun, before whom he had to lose all his audacity; and finally Saturn, where he became entitled to be called 'Father'. As the incarnation of the divine, he then received the experience of knowing the transcendent wonder of his true nature. Among the ordeals he had passed triumphantly through were likely to have been fasting, scourging, branding and tests of heat and cold.[81,66]

When Mithraism was adopted by the Romans, it was the soldiers for whom it held the greatest appeal. They carried its beliefs all over the western world and altars to Mithra are found at many Roman camps. The Imperial cult of Sol Invictus (supreme Sun-god) was officially syncretised with Mithraism by Aurelian in 270 AD.

When the new Christianity came into being, there was some confusion at first for the stories of the two world saviours bear startling similarities. One of the reasons for this may have been the influence of the Persians on Christianity in Italy during the first century. Mithra, entering the world beside a sacred stream and beneath a sacred tree, was thought to be archetypal Man, born from the virgin Earth. His birth took place on 25 December and was witnessed by shepherds. At the end of his period of incarnation he held a last supper with his disciples and then returned to heaven. It was believed that he would come again to earth when the world came to an end. After the final victorious battle with darkness and evil, he would judge those to be resurrected and would lead them through a river of fire to immortality. It was believed imperative to prepare for this second coming by devoting one's life to him; and, as we have seen, it was also believed possible to have communion with him through the stages of initiation.

New Christians found themselves bewildered by the similarities between the two deities and decided that Mithra must be a creation of Satan sent to mock Christ (although Mithra preceded Christ by many centuries). Satan was the Christian equivalent of Ahriman, the Persian cosmic power of darkness and deceit. The Romans preferred Mithra to Christ for a long time but eventually he was driven out by the Christians.

Campbell has noted a fundamental difference in the world views of Mithraism and Christianity. Christianity shares with

Persian Zoroastrianism, from whence Mithra arose, the dualistic belief that time began and time will end, that evil exists and must be overcome by good, that the not-of-this-world God reveals himself in historical events, and that to accord with God's will the world must 'progress' and not stay still. In contrast, the Hellenised Mithraism of the fourth century BCE did not believe in historical boundaries of time, but in timelessness. This understanding was expressed in an aspect of Mithra – a lion-headed, naked man twined around seven times by a serpent whose head rests above the man's brow. He was Zervan Akarana – Boundless Time – and on his back were four wings showing the seasons of the year. In each hand he held a key and on his chest lay a thunderbolt, symbol of illumination.[34]

The importance of Zervan Akarana (often equated with the Greek Dionysus and the Hindu Vishnu, the Man-Lion) was that he represented a total reversal of religious emphasis from the Christian. In a timeless world the notion of progress is meaningless. Instead it is change (as the seasons change) which is the fact to be accepted. In Hellenic Mithraism it was not a life-improving but a life-affirming attitude – a celebration of life as it was – which enabled the hero to accept the necessity of death and even to celebrate it in the bull sacrifice. Death itself, in all its blood and horror, was to be affirmed and not denied for it was part of the nature of existence.

The biographical details of Mithra and Christ were very close and obviously derive from the same source, yet they 'represent a completely different reading of the nature of the universe and of man: a mystical affirmation against a moral corrective, and a reassertion of the elder, primitive, and generally pagan designation of the sacrifice.'[34]

And yet Mithra was a 'saviour' of mankind, as was Christ. If all was to be affirmed, what could be the role of a saviour? The answer lies in the understanding (found in Buddhism and implicit in Hellenism) that on the earthly level there is such a thing as evil which must be overcome; but on a higher level evil has no substantive reality but is merely the opposite of an equally unreal 'good'.

ISIS, MOTHER OF EGYPT

Egypt was the essence of exotic fascination to the Romans, its religion even more ancient than the Greek. By the first century AD the Egyptian goddess Isis was widely worshipped throughout the empire, even as far as its limits in Britain, where a temple was dedicated to her.

Isis was one of the most enduring, endearing and beautiful expressions of the Mother Goddess that humanity has ever believed in. Her story (going back to 3000 BCE) is one that emphasises all the feminine qualities of noble protectress, wise administrator, and loyal wife and mother. She and her brother-husband, Osiris, were renowned rulers of Egypt who brought civilisation to the country. Isis taught the women to spin and weave, to grind corn and to cure illnesses. When Osiris departed on his peaceful conquest of the world, she took his place in governing Egypt, which she managed with great ability. But her heart was broken when she learnt of the death of Osiris, killed by his violent brother Set. She cut off her hair, changed her robes for common ones and voyaged down the Nile in search of the coffin in which the remains of Osiris had been placed. But the coffin, hard-heartedly thrown by Set into the Nile, had been washed out to sea and eventually came to rest on the Phoenician coast beside a tamarisk tree.

The tree, newly nourished, grew so quickly that it incorporated the coffin into its trunk. The king of Byblos, hearing of this amazingly huge tree, ordered it to be cut down to make a prop for the roof of his palace. When this was done the tree began to give off so wonderful a fragrance that news of it reached Isis, who at once understood its significance and set off for Phoenicia. To cut a long shory short, she was given the coffin from the trunk. She took it home and hid it in a swamp so that Set would not hear about it. By chance, however, he discovered it and this time he cut up the body of his brother into fourteen pieces and scattered them far and wide. Isis patiently searched for and found all the pieces except for the phallus, which had been eaten by a Nile crab (cursed to this day).

She cunningly bound the body together, substituting an artificial phallus. Then, for the first time in Egyptian history, she performed the rite of embalmment, which brought her murdered husband back to immortal life. From his embrace she conceived a son, Horus, who grew up to be the embodiment of noble virtues, his life protected by her magical powers.

Isis, according to Graves,[73] represented the fruitful plains of Egypt while Osiris was the fertilising Nile which inundated them and Set was the arid desert, always a threat. But the Greek historian Plutarch might have disagreed: 'Indeed all men have Isis and know her and the Gods of her company; . . . they should take very good heed and be apprehensive lest unwittingly they write-off the sacred mysteries and dissolve them into winds and streams, and sowing and ploughings, and passions of earth and changes of seasons.'[82]

It was as a healing goddess, as one who could apply the balm of love and thus reconstruct and put together things which had fallen apart, that Isis was adored. Gradually she absorbed many of the other goddesses, both Greek and Roman, and her cult lasted well into the sixth century AD. Great festivals took place in her honour. She was both moon-goddess and goddess of waters and navigation, and one of the big rituals of the spring festival was the procession of her ships down the Nile. These processions were described by Apuleius, who also revealed that there were secret ceremonies of initiation belonging to her cult.

Sacred to Isis was the cow and she is sometimes shown with a disc headdress set between cow's horns; or as a cow's head set on a human body. But more often she is depicted beside Osiris, holding him – as she holds all the dead whom she takes across the waters – with her winged arms. And she is often shown holding the god-infant Horus, resembling in her attitude the divine compassion of Mary with Jesus. Indeed, ancient statues of Isis suckling her child have been taken over by Catholic communities who have mistaken her for their own Madonna. It seems more than likely that some of the shrines to the Black Virgin in Europe have developed from the Black Isis, particularly since she was believed to be Mother of God and was worshipped as a virgin, just as were all the other moon-goddesses.

She appeared to Apuleius, her devotee, and he describes her in The Golden Ass:

I am she that is the natural mother of all things, mistress and governess of all the elements, the initial progeny of worlds, chief of the powers divine, queen of all that are in hell, the principal of them that dwell in heaven, manifested alone and under one form of all the gods and goddesses. At my will the planets of the sky, the wholesome winds of the seas, and the lamentable silences of hell are disposed; my name, my divinity is adored throughout the world, in divers manners, in variable customs, and by many names.[82]

THE BEAR-SHAPED GODDESS

A tradition in Greece which must have had its origin in Cro-Magnon times, if not earlier, was that of a goddess in the shape of a bear, a Bear-Mother, known in Crete even today as 'Virgin Mary of the Bear'. During the last centuries BCE, when the ancient Great Goddess was surviving under many names, she appeared as the bear-shaped goddess Artemis, mistress of wild animals and of all that lives untamed within mankind. She was both uncaptured Virgin and Mother, protector of the weak. She is usually shown surrounded by her animals and nymphs. In Rome she was called Diana, the Virgin Huntress of the wildwood. She was to be found in all natural places – forests, hills and valleys – and would appear as a doe or bear. She was often linked with the stag and she played with bulls.

Dressed as bears, Athenian girls danced in her honour, and in a mystery initiation were 'possessed' by bears. They offered phalli to Artemis, as well as crops and animal sacrifices. Because she was a fertility goddess it was believed that sacrifice was essential and goats, stags and hares (the moon) were considered particularly appropriate.

It was also believed that she appeared at childbirth in her role of Bear-Mother, caring for the newly born with all the protectiveness of a she-bear. Yet she was not fully a compassionate Earth Mother who receives life back to herself, for 'she reflects the virginity of nature with all its brilliance and wildness, with its guiltless purity and its strangeness. And yet intertwined with this crystal-clear essence were the dark roots of savage nature. Artemis . . . aroused madness. Her anger caused the death of women in childbirth.'[82]

In this double-natured role (so often attributed to goddesses) she resembles Kali of India, although Kali's nature was even more deadly. But her worship throughout Europe was universal, either as Artemis or Diana.

DIONYSUS, THE GOD OF WINE AND LOVE

Another god of nature was Dionysus, also known as Bacchus by the Romans. He was a fertility god, directly connected with the seasons and with trees. Miracles accompanied him to do with water and with the sap of vegetation. Streams gushed from rocks and rivers filled with milk and honey. Empty bowls were found to contain wine and vines produced both flowers and grapes in a day.

His story has all the strange symbolism of the spiritual journey, for he was twice-born. His first birth was to Zeus and Persephone – the great Sky god and the daughter of the Earth Mother. But Dionysus became entranced with his own face in a mirror when he was a child and was seized by the Titans, the giants who created the physical world. They tore him to pieces and ate all his flesh except for his heart, which was saved by Athene. Zeus threw his thunderbolts at the Titans and burnt them to ashes. From these ashes – which contained the essence of Dionysus, for each had devoured a portion of him – the human race was created. Thus every human has a touch of Dionysus in the psyche.

A love-potion was prepared from the preserved heart of the child and this was given to Semele, a mortal woman, daughter of the King of Thebes. Semele was in love with Zeus and became pregnant by him. The potion caused her to beg him to reveal himself to her in all his Olympian splendour. But when he obeyed she could not endure his fearful brilliance and was burnt to death by the flames of his body. Zeus took the unborn child into his thigh and when it was time for it to come forth he drew it out. In this way Dionysus was born again.[66]

Dionysus is believed to represent the mind of the universe – its idea. The Titans had put together the fragments of the world but it was Dionysus who created them into a whole. To be in the highest state of Dionysian consciousness meant to know oneself in the profoundest sense, whereas to be in the Titanic state was to have lost the awareness of oneself and to be fragmented throughout one's world, unconscious of its intrinsic oneness.[71]

There were twelve Titans, thought to be analogous to the zodiac, and when they dismembered Dionysus it was because they had become over-involved in the world they had brought together. It is believed that Dionysus also represented the sun, who is nightly dismembered by the zodiac, and from whose body the universe was formed. But when humanity was created from the Titanic ashes, its sense of oneness was lost and a sense of separateness begun.

Typically, Dionysus was brought up on a mountainside, for the mountain has an age-old connection with the spiritual journey. As a young man, he travelled to India, carrying with him the Greek civilisation, and to Egypt and Libya. When he returned to Greece he was changed, having become softer and less manly. He was

> a foreigner, a preacher, a sorcerer . . . with beautiful perfumed curls, rosy cheeks, and in his eyes the grace of Aphrodite. Under the pretext of teaching the sweet and charming practices of the *evoe*, he corrupts girls. Women are inspired to forsake their houses and run about the mountains by night, dancing to the music of tabors and flutes.[58]

In Thebes he was thrown into prison and his revenge was to strike the Theban women with madness so that the king's mother murdered her own son in a frenzy. This horrific event is the subject of Euripides' play *The Bacchae*.

Eventually Dionysus regained his divinity and all his popularity. This was partly because he had absorbed foreign gods into his persona, as well as many rural divinities such as Pan. And it was also because he was credited with discovering the grape and his festivals came to be associated with joyful wine-drinking and processions through sunlit glades. To a large extent the early ideal of Dionysus was replaced by a more self-indulgent version.

The cult of Dionysus was a great and influential one. It included all his retinue of satyrs – spirits of the woods and mountains who combined the characteristics of a male goat with a human body; centaurs – whose body and head were those of a man but who travelled on four horse-legs; and nymphs – young and beautiful deities of streams, forests and mountains. The oak tree was sacred to the nymphs and they wore garlands of oak leaves.

Closely associated with Dionysus and part of his retinue was the wild god of the woods, Pan. Pan was born with the legs, horns and beard of a goat and for a long time he inhabited the mountains of Arcadia where his sudden appearances would cause such fright to travellers that these scares came to be called *panics*. But every rural region of Greece had its own Pan, a phallic god who promoted fertility and roamed the forests, sporting with nymphs. Images of Pan have been found in every part of Europe, showing how popular he was in country minds.

As part of the cult of Dionysus, Pan shared in the mystery rites associated with that wine-loving god. The rites themselves reflect the two aspects of Dionysus' being – his higher mind and his earth-consciousness. There is something familiar to most of us in Dionysus, for he symbolised both creative order and the irrational, both the mindful and the uncontrolled – perhaps because his father was a god and his mother a human. He came to be associated with the bull, brimming with virility and adored by women. Phalli were used as signposts for ceremonial routes, and at his yearly festivals each woman carried one. The true worshipper ate the raw flesh of the bull and women wore horns in imitation of his bull-headed self – for Dionysus as bull-god represented the wisdom of man combined with the strength and virility of the bull.

In some ways he resembles that most mysterious of all Indian gods, Shiva, who was also to be found scattering seeds in the forests while riding on a bull, and who danced a life-dance of joy while also delivering death. He shared with Dionysus the phallus as the symbol of his cult.

The rites of Dionysus (also known as the rites of Bacchus) were, at their highest level, to lift the soul out of its Titanic, irrational and separated state and to draw it into the state of oneness and clarity. But at the other levels the rites seem to preclude the possibility of that enlightened state. The popular rites were celebrated at night on mountainsides or in forest glades. The sacrificial victim (an animal) was believed to be Dionysus himself and was torn to pieces alive. As the bits were eaten, communion with the god was realised. This resulted in an ecstasy which carried the participant far away from any human limitations. It was an ecstatic frenzy in which all humanness was dropped and anything became possible. Freedom to be the delivered self was accompanied by freedom from all rules and conventions. In some way unknown to us today, the eating of raw flesh brought back the ancient patterns of life, that which was known hundreds of thousands of years ago. And even more, it brought about a feeling of communion with the underlying force of the cosmos itself.

Many considered such moments of ecstatic possession as madness and Dionysus has always been associated with the mad. 'But what distinguishes Dionysus and his cult is not these psychopathic crises *but the fact that they were valorised as religious experience*, whether as a punishment or as a favour from the god.'[68] Eliade tells us that he is the only Greek god who,

> revealing himself under different aspects, dazzles and attracts both peasants and the intellectual elite, politicians and contemplatives, orgiastics and ascetics. Intoxication, eroticism, universal fertility, but also the unforgettable experiences inspired by the periodic arrival of the dead, or by *mania*, by immersion in animal unconsciousness, or by the ecstasy of *enthousiasmos* – all these terrors and revelations spring from a single source: *the presence of the god*. His mode of being expresses the paradoxical unity of life and death. This is why Dionysus constitutes a type of divinity radically different from the Olympians. Was he *nearer* to human beings than the other gods? In any case, one could approach him, could even incorporate him and the ecstasy of *mania* proved that the human condition could be surpassed.[58]

Nevertheless, even if the madness or frenzy – which came to be called 'being filled with the god' – did break apart human boundaries and allow people to share together in a shattering experience of intoxicating spontaneous activity, it did not appear to lead to transcendence. Nor did it seem to lead to the clarity and sanity of true illumination, although in some sense that may have been its aim. Perhaps we can agree with Joscelyn Godwin that 'what is certain is that one insists at one's peril on fitting the Dionysian phenomena into a single, unifying theory of religious experience, substituting a tidy intellectual construct for a reality as vivid, as varied, and as unruly as the world itself.'[71]

THE ARCHETYPAL MESSENGERS

A host of other gods and goddesses made their appearance in western Europe in the first centuries AD. Their roles were not antagonistic, rather they influenced and enriched each other, for they conferred the ability to sense and experience life itself as divine. There was a large degree of syncretism – one god incorporating another – for at no time were people troubled by the possessive idea that only one deity could convey the truth. Thus there developed throughout a large area of the world – from Scotland to Africa and eastwards to India – what Campbell has called

> a single, rich and colourful religious empire with an infinite wealth of forms, joining and harmonising on many levels with all the pantheons of the nations: Celtic, Germanic, Roman, Greek, and Oriental. . . . The function of these cults was to bring about, by one means or another, a psychological transformation in the candidate for knowledge, as a result of which his mind should come to rest in the realisation that divinity inheres in, as well as transcends, every particle of the universe and all its beings.[34]

People need archetypes to inspire their lives. Such an archetype as Osiris, the god who dies and is restored to life, was a personal and significant symbol of immortality. By identifying with the god, the believer could share in his life-enhancing qualities. For the gods and goddesses, warm and living, were expressions of inspiration rather than commandments written on stone. They gave hope and confidence to those who needed such sustaining qualities. Perhaps people longed foolishly – and may still long – for a magical hero who would conquer all obstacles and set everything right. But another, more profound longing, was for the unifying blessings of mercy and deliverance which, through commitment to the initiations and perfections of the deities, the courageous were able to find.

Cicero himself wrote of the mystery religions:

> Among the many excellent and divine institutions that your Athens has developed and contributed to human life, there is

none, in my opinion, better than these mysteries, by which we have been brought forth from our rustic and savage mode of existence, cultivated, and refined to a state of civilisation: and as the rites are called 'initiations', so, in truth, we have learned from them the first principles of life and have gained the understanding, not only to live happily, but also to die with better hope.[45]

CHAPTER NINE
The war gods of the north

The Roman world crumbled and fell. By the fifth century AD, Rome was beset by enemies without and by the weakness of her emperors within. The Germanic tribes that had been merely a border nuisance in the heyday of Rome, barbarians on the outskirts of the empire, came rushing in when Rome collapsed to seize the rich lands which could no longer be defended. A great turmoil of land-hungry migrations took place between the fourth and sixth centuries. The Germanic Franks, Vandals, Visigoths and Ostrogoths advanced over the continent, while Britain was invaded by Angles and Saxons from across the North Sea.

Wherever the Germanic peoples went they took their fierce beliefs with them. Although there had been trade and commerce with Rome from earliest times, the Germanic gods had never been threatened by the Romans. As they did with the Celts, the Romans took a genuine and friendly interest in the strange northern religion on their borders, and Tacitus did his best to equate some of the Germanic gods with Roman equivalents.

In fact it is through Tacitus, writing in the second century AD, that we learn about the early gods of the northerners, for this was long before the fall of Rome and there was leisure and opportunity to travel and study. As well, Tacitus may have learnt much from the visit to Rome of the king of a tribe called the Semnones, who lived between the Rhine and the Oder.

Tacitus tells us that the Germanic people were very warlike and that they had a particular battle-cry – 'a harsh piercing note and a broken roar'[155] – which they magnified by pressing their mouths to their shields. This would have had the effect of spreading the sound all about, to confuse the enemy. Like the Celts, they went into battle naked 'or lightly covered with a small mantle'. But unlike the Celts, they took no pride in their equipment and merely painted their shields rather than engraving them. On the whole, Tacitus thought them a crude lot, although protective of their women. He noted, 'They even suppose somewhat of sanctity and prescience to be inherent in the female sex; and therefore neither despise their counsels, nor disregard their responses.'[156]

Tacitus was also impressed by the importance the Germans gave to divination. They used a twig from a fruit tree which was divided into small pieces, each cut with a certain mark, known as a rune. These were then thrown at random on to a white cloth. The priest, after an invocation to the gods, would pick up in succession three pieces and interpret their significance according to the rune each had on it. They also (like the Celts) divined their fate from the flight and calls of wild birds. But unlike the Celts, they used horses too as a means of naming destiny. 'Milk-white and untouched by earthly labour', the horses were kept in a sacred wood. When an omen was needed, they would be yoked to a consecrated chariot and led out by the priest or the king – 'who attentively observes their neighing and snorting: and no kind of augury is more credited, not only among the people, but among the nobles and priests. For the priests consider themselves as ministers of the gods, and the horses as revealing the divine will.'[156]

The Celts may have seemed fierce, but the Germans craved war.

> If their native country be long sunk in peace and inaction, many of the young nobles repair to some other state then engaged in war. . . . The noble requires from his chief the warlike steed, the bloody and conquering spear: and in place of pay, he expects to be supplied with food, homely indeed, but plentiful. The funds for this munificence must be found in war and rapine; nor are they so easily persuaded to cultivate the earth, and await the produce of the seasons, as to challenge the foe, and expose themselves to wounds; nay, they even think it baseless and spiritless to earn by sweat what they might purchase with their blood.[156]

This blood-loving attitude was reflected in their gods. Tacitus mentions two in particular. One was Woden and the other was Tiwaz (Tiw or Tig in Britain), whom Tacitus equated with Mercury. Woden, he decided, was the northern form of Mars. Both Woden and Tiwaz were violent gods of battle.

Tacitus learnt from the king of the Semnones that this tribe gathered together once a year in a sacred wood where they watched a human sacrifice. Whoever came into the wood had to be tied with a cord to make him humble before the god – perhaps as a sign that he was *tied to the god* – and if he fell over he was not allowed to get on to his feet again but had to advance rolling over the ground. This belief in tying or binding occurs throughout the history of the northern war gods. The god in this case seems to have been Tiwaz. All the forcefulness and determination of the Germanic peoples seems to have been fully expressed in their deities. Little of the poetic dreaminess of the Celts could find space to exist when it came up against the Germanic religion. Even more than from the Romans, the Celts fled from the Goths and the Anglo-Saxons.

For Woden, as well as being the god of war, was also lord of the kingdom of death. His name means 'one who makes mad'. There was a belief that he should be fed on blood and so blood continually had to be found, necessitating constant warfare. Not only were streams of flowing blood to be obtained but, as well, all the accoutrements of war, such as shields, spears and mantles, must be thrown into swamps or rivers or burnt in a pyre to the honour of Woden after every battle.

Tacitus noted that the Germans had only one public spectacle – young men dancing naked amongst drawn swords and spears. He thought them a quarrelsome but sincere people: 'The frequent quarrels that arise amongst them, when intoxicated, seldom terminate in abusive language, but more frequently in blood.'[156] But in their favour, he added, 'These people, naturally void of artifice or disguise, disclose the most secret emotions of their hearts in the freedom of feasting.'[156] Nevertheless he found them without much style or elegance, even their funerals 'without parade'. The only occasion of a ritual nature was when the body of an eminent person was burnt in a fire of special woods. But, as we shall see, even this uninspiring and savage religion was to produce gods which were worshipped throughout Europe. This was due not so much to the intrinsic worth of the deities as to the fervour with which they were upheld, first by the Germans and then by the Vikings.

THE CONQUERING VIKINGS

By the seventh century, Christianity had largely converted the Germanic peoples, including the Anglo-Saxons, to itself – at least on the surface. Temples were replaced by churches and crosses arose everywhere. But in Scandinavia the old Germanic religion reigned triumphant, fiercely repelling Christianity until at least the tenth or eleventh centuries. It is thus from Scandinavia, particularly from Norway and Sweden, that we learn about the northern gods, and we do so through the authorship of a brilliant thirteenth-century Icelander, Snorri Sturluson. He decided to write an account of the old religion before all its descriptions in sagas and verses were lost. He himself was a Christian and Christianity was by then widespread. But he was also a poet and historian and a lover of the fine and true. He planned his book as a guide to poets and he told the stories of the gods with a vivid wit and real understanding of their nature and purpose. His work was called the *Edda* – the *Prose Edda* for his stories and the *Verse Edda* for his translations – and it is to the *Edda* that we turn for our knowledge.

Between the eighth and eleventh centuries the Vikings were the scourge of the western world (opinion nowadays tries to make of them mere traders but this can hardly be credited). A proud, fierce, indomitable people from Norway, Sweden, and Denmark, they bore down on villages and churches in France, Spain, Germany and Britain, burning and plundering, raping and killing. They came in long-boats by sea and at one time it looked as if they would conquer the west and bring an end to Christianity. They were the rulers of the Hebrides, Orkneys and Shetlands as well as some of southern Ireland, including Dublin. Columba's monastery on Iona was sacked and the monks massacred, as was Lindisfarne, an international centre of learning. Hamburg and Paris were plundered and so were Cadiz and Seville. They reached down the Dnieper to the Black Sea and crossed the Atlantic to the east coast of America. Northern and eastern England were theirs and only the wisdom of Alfred the Great prevented southern England falling to them too.

The northern gods, whose worship had been carried all over Europe by the earlier Germanic people, had never been forgotten.

Whatever impact Christianity had made it was certainly never a total one. Now their worship was brought to the fore again by the Vikings and throughout Europe the old beliefs skirmished with the new.

For an account of what the northerners believed in, we can do no better than go to Snorri:

> In the beginning, there was but a Yawning Gap. In the north, then, the frigid Mist-World appeared, in the midst of which there was a well, from which the world rivers flowed. In the south appeared the world of heat, glowing, burning and impassable to such as have not their holdings there. And those frigid streams from the north, pressing toward the south, sent up a yeasty venom that hardened to ice, which halted, and the mist congealed to rime. And when the breath of southern heat met the rime, it melted, dripped, and life was quickened from the yeast drops in the form of a great sleeping giant Ymir.
>
> A sweat came over Ymir and there grew under his left hand a male and female, one of his feet begat a son with the other, and thus the Rime Giants appeared. Moreover, there condensed from the rime a cow, her name Audumla, four streams of milk flowing from her udder; and she nourished Ymir. She licked the ice-blocks, which were salty, and the first day she licked, hair appeared on the blocks; the next day, a man's head; and the next, the whole man was there. His name was Buri, fair of feature, great and mighty.
>
> Buri begat Borr, who married the daughter of a giant and had three sons, Othin, Vili and Ve, who slew the giant Ymir and fashioned of his body the earth: of his blood the sea and waters, land of his flesh, crags of his bones, gravel and stones from his teeth and broken bones; heaven they made of his skull, set over the earth, and under each corner they set a dwarf; fire and sparks from the south they scattered, some to wander in the sky, others to stand fixed, and so were made the sun, moon and stars. And the earth was circular, with the deep sea round about. They assigned the outer edge of the earth to the giants; for the inward part they made a great citadel round about the world: and they called this Midgard. Of Ymir's brain they made the clouds. And they fashioned

men and women of two trees to which they gave spirit and life, wit and feeling, and then form, speech, hearing and sight, clothing and name. Moreover, in the middle of the world they fashioned a city for themselves, of which there are many tidings and tales. Othin sat there on high, his wife was Frigg; and their race is the race known as Aesir. All-father he is called, because he is the father of all the gods and of men, and of all that was fulfilled of him and of his might.[157]

YGGDRASIL THE WORLD-TREE

Othin, more commonly known as Odin, was the Scandinavian name for the Germanic Woden. He was the greatest of the gods and his horse browsed on the foliage of the World-Tree, Yggdrasil. This vast ash tree stood in the centre of the earth and spread its branches all over the world. It rose from three roots. One root reached down to the underworld, the Mist-World, from which all the waters flowed. Another root penetrated the world of the Rime Giants and beside it was the miraculous well of Mimir (memory and knowledge) covered with frost and ice, in which dwelt all wisdom. It was to drink from these waters that Odin sacrificed an eye: 'The Allfather came there looking for a draught from the well, but he didn't get it until he had put one of his eyes in pawn.'[25] According to Brian Branston, this was not really about Odin so much as about the ancient sky father, the Sun, whose disappearance every night was symbolised by the pledged eye which was swallowed up by the waters of the ocean – or Mimir's well.[25]

The third root was in the land of the gods, Aesir, and by it was to be found another well, a holy one tended by three sisters, the Norns. The wisest of these sisters was called Wyrd, with which weaving is connected, for she was the greatest of the three Fate sisters and her role as the weaver whose thread was the destinies of men was believed in for many centuries. In the Anglo-Saxon epic *Beowulf*, 'the Lord gave the people webs to speed them in their battles'[15] and Wyrd in particular was believed to influence the course of battle. The name-meanings of the three sisters were Fate, Being and Necessity. Each day they pasted the Ash Tree with a mixture of holy well water and sacred clay, the result being as white as an egg shell.

On the highest branch of the Tree an eagle kept eternal vigilance while beneath the Tree, at the Aesir root, a malevolent serpent continually gnawed and nibbled at it in an attempt to bring the Tree down. The serpent was at war with the eagle and an agile squirrel ran up and down the Tree carrying insults from one to the other. Four stags wandered among the branches and ate the new shoots. But the Norns were there to protect the Tree from real destruction.

Trees have always been deeply interwoven with the human psyche. There is something about a tree's protective power and strong beauty which touches us at a profound level. The symmetry of the branches and fresh soft green of the leaves carry us into a luminous realm. The very height of a tree adds essential perspective to the landscape, as those who live in the new treeless areas of grain cultivation must have discovered to their cost. The mystical bond between tree and human goes back into immeasurable time, perhaps because many trees outlive individual lives and seem to be eternal in their ability to 'die' and be resurrected. Such inexhaustible life was to the Germanic peoples an expression of ultimate reality, and the Tree as the centre of the world was the symbol of that reality. 'A tree becomes sacred, while continuing to be a tree, because of the power it expresses; and if it becomes a cosmic tree, it is because what it expressed is a perfect reproduction of what the cosmos expresses.'[63]

Yggdrasil, then, is a cosmic ideogram, to be read as the whole of life manifested in tree form. It is not the tree itself which is sacred so much as the transcendent reality which it signifies.

> By being consecrated, the individual 'profane' plant species is transubstantiated; in the dialectic of the sacred a part (a tree, a plant) has the value of the whole (the cosmos, life), a profane thing becomes a hierophany. Yggdrasil was the symbol of the Universe, but to the Germans of old any oak (or ash) tree could become sacred if it partook of the archetypal condition, if it 'repeated' Yggdrasil.[63]

VALHALLA THE WARRIOR'S HEAVEN

After the forming of heaven and earth, the realm of the gods was built – Asgard. Here were great halls in which the gods dwelt. Odin, leader of them all, had two halls. The one in which he resided was built of spears and the roof was lined with silver shields; from it he could behold all the worlds at once. His other hall was Valhalla, familiar in legend as the haven of the slain where all who had been killed in battle could find rest and hospitality. Each night an endless supply of roast pork was served and from the udders of a goat which browsed on Yggdrasil there flowed mead instead of milk. The hall itself contained 550 doors, each one wide enough for 800 warriors to march through at one time.

Odin took it upon himself to visit the battlefields of the world each day and to bring back with him those warriors who had fallen, to be restored in Valhalla. In this task he was helped by the Valkyries, strong maidens who could carry the dead and who were empowered to choose those to be slain. Before they reached Valhalla, however, the newly dead must wade through the howling Thund, the River of Air. Safely past it, they could enter Valhalla, but only by one door, the outermost entry, called Valgrind, 'the holy barred-gate of the slain'. In the morning, resurrected, the warriors were returned to battle, and thus their whole lives were spent in battle and feasting. Snorri translates the *Verse Edda* to tell us:

> All the Einheriar
> in Odin's barracks
>   crack each other's crowns every day;
> they bundle up the dead
> ride back from the fight . . .
>   and down sit to drink all healed.[25]

Valhalla was thus the heaven for warriors engaged in eternal battle. They were called the adopted sons of Odin – himself Valfather, or 'Father of the Slain' – and they had the name of Champions. In this atmosphere 'heroic death became a preferred religious experience'.[58]

The idea of unceasing battle is not one which appeals to us today. Although we live under the immense threat of extinction by nuclear disaster, the hand-to-hand fighting of past ages has little attraction or even reality for those of us lucky enough not to live in the Middle East, Northern Ireland, or parts of the Third

World. And even in those strife-torn areas, the impersonality of a gun cuts the user off from the fearlessness he would have had to display in olden days.

Most of us cannot know, therefore, the first-hand experience of fighting as it was practised then. There was glory attached to the battle and the warrior accepted the risks and fears as part of the natural order. Although he submitted his will to that of his leader, yet he was still an individual fighting an individual enemy. Love of such a heightened experience, perhaps equal to that of a religious frenzy, seems to have swept the Germanic peoples and the Scandinavians into orgies of massacre. Belief in Valhalla meant, in fact, believing that the battle would never stop, for the warrior, restored to life, would go back to the thick of it.

ODIN AND THE BERSERKS

The choosers of the slain, the Valkyries, were the 'friends of Odin', and the great figure of the father-god is the key to the blood-lust of his followers.

Odin was not only the god of war but also of intelligence. He was endowed with a silver tongue which made whatever he said seem true to his hearer. He had the shamanic power to change shape into animal or bird and his very approach was able to strike his enemies blind, deaf or impotent. He was said to wander through the battleground and sap the willpower of the enemy by his very presence.

But more formidable was his army of berserks – and it is here that we sense blood-madness and frenzy. According to Snorri, the berserks 'were frantic as dogs or wolves; they bit their shields and were as strong as bears or boars; they slew men, but neither fire nor iron could hurt them. This is known as "running berserk".'[151]

The berserks were not just legendary figures but were given status in society as a special class, free from ordinary laws. In the first century, Tacitus describes a group of dedicated warriors, the Catti, who let their hair grow and did not cut it until they had slain an enemy:

> over blood and spoils they unveil the countenance [draw back the hair] and proclaim that they have at length paid the debt of

> existence, and have proved themselves worthy of their country and parents. The cowardly and effeminate continue in their squalid disguise. The bravest among them wear also an iron ring (a mark of ignominy in that nation) as a kind of chain, till they have released themselves by the slaughter of a foe.

Another group noted by Tacitus, called the Arii,

> improve their natural ferocity of aspect by artificial helps. Their shields are black, their bodies painted black: they choose the darkest nights for an attack; and strike terror by the funereal gloom of their sable bands – no enemy being able to sustain their singular and, as it were, infernal appearance; since in every combat the eyes are the first subdued.[156]

As late as the ninth century there was a section of berserks in the bodyguard of King Harald Fairhair of Norway, and it may well be that the Vikings emulated the berserks, or included groups of them. The berserk initiation to serve with King Harald is thought to have been the touching of a spear consecrated to Odin. This ceremony would have given them the assurance of immortality in Odin's service. Groups of berserks were known to have wandered, scavenging, throughout Scandinavia and were thought to be magic shape-shifters, able to take animal form when the frenzy of rage turned them into wild beasts.[53]

The ecstasy of battle which filled the berserks with madness, so that they knew neither fear nor pain, was thought of as a particular gift from Odin. And here we can see the link with Woden, who was known as 'the one who makes mad'. But Odin was also called the Great Deceiver. For madness alone is not a guarantee against injury and a berserk might well come to and find himself irreparably wounded. Thus Odin had his untrustworthy side and in battle could be capricious as to whom he saved or betrayed.[25]

It is not known whether the shamanic sacred mushroom, the *amanita muscaria*, was used in the creation of the blood frenzy – perhaps not, since there is no specific reference to it. It may be that the berserks felt they did not need it since they were possessed by Odin and could work that possession up into a maniacal condition – which in itself would probably bring victory.

ODIN AS SHAMAN

There is some evidence that Odin was a real person. There is a probability that he was originally a shaman chieftain from the north-east who migrated to Scandinavia and set up a kingdom, taking to himself the name of Odin. Sigge, the chief of an Asiatic tribe, is said to have emigrated to Sweden where he

> built Sigtuna as the capital of his empire, and promulgated a new code of laws, and established the sacred mysteries. He, himself, assumed the name of Odin, and founded the priesthood of the twelve Drottars who conducted the secret worship, and the administration of justice, and, as prophets, revealed the future. The secret rites of these mysteries celebrated the death of Balder, the beautiful and lovely, and represented the grief of Gods and men at his death, and his restoration to life.[81]

The Odinic mystery cult held its ceremonies in underground crypts. The initiate was given the task of raising the beautiful, murdered god Balder, youngest son of Odin, from the dead. The initiate, although he did not know it, was himself playing the part of Balder.

> He called himself a wanderer; the caverns through which he passed were symbolic of the worlds and spheres of Nature. The priests who initiated him were emblematic of the sun, the moon, and the stars. . . .
>
> After wandering for hours through the intricate passageways, the candidate was ushered into the presence of a statue of Balder the Beautiful, the prototype of all initiates into the Mysteries. This figure stood in the centre of a great apartment roofed with shields. In the midst of the chamber stood a plant with seven blossoms, emblematic of the planets. In this room, which symbolised the house of the Aesir, or Wisdom, the neophyte took his oath of secrecy and piety upon the naked blade of a sword. He drank the sanctified mead from a bowl made of a human skull and, having passed successfully through all the tortures and trials designed to divert him from the course of wisdom, he was finally permitted to unveil the

> mystery of Odin – the personification of wisdom. He was presented, in the name of Balder, with the sacred ring of the order; he was hailed as a man reborn; and it was said of him that he had died and had been raised again without passing through the gates of death.[81]

Shamanism too was an essential ingredient of Odin-worship and the mysteries. Odin's eight-legged horse Sleipnir, with its ability to carry him through the air, is characteristic of a shaman's steed; while his ravens, Thought and Memory, who flew over the world each day, represent the journey of the mind – although the ravens, like Odin's wolves Ravener and Greed, were also devourers of the dead.

In the *Edda* poem 'Baldrs Draumar', Sleipnir carries Odin in a typical shaman's journey down to the underworld, to the region of the goddess, Hel, in order to consult a dead seeress – thus showing his ability to speak with the dead. The seeress seems to answer against her will:

> Who is this man, unknown to me,
> Who drives me on down this weary path?

In spite of her unwillingness, Odin continues to question her, prefacing every query with a plea: 'Be not silent, volva,' to which she continually reiterates, 'I have spoken unwillingly: now I must be silent.' Other poems contain a similar refrain and they could be seen as the shaman's unwilling speech on coming out of his trance after the journey of his soul to the underworld.[53]

Like his earlier self, Woden, Odin was able to paralyse the minds of men in battle or release them from their battle tensions and bestow fearlessness by his gift of war-frenzy. Ellis Davidson tells us of memorial stones where a 'walknut' is depicted beside the carved figure of Odin. A walknut was a knot, similar to the Celtic triskele. The walknut was thought to be the symbol of that binding and unbinding power.[53]

The name of Odin was, like Woden, associated with the wind. As god of the dead, he was believed to lead the 'wild hunt', the procession of dead souls riding through the air which could be heard passing by in the storm. Great terror was inspired by this image which came to be seen as the unchaining of all the brute forces in the world, and the Christians believed Odin to be the devil. Pictures of him show him as vastly tall and thin, wearing a long cloak and with tangled grey hair falling about him. His fierce face with an open gaping eye-socket is shadowed by a wide-brimmed hat. He is accompanied by his raven and wolf, and leans on a blackthorn staff.[81]

Odin was credited with all the shaman's abilities of divining the future, knowing the reasons for calamities, and raising the dead. He was also able to bring ecstasy, a shamanic gift. The Scandinavian derivation of his name means 'raging, furious, intoxicated'. This description 'can be used to signify poetic genius and inspiration. Such meanings are most appropriate for the name of a god who not only inspired the battle fury of the berserks, but also obtained the mead of inspiration for the Aesir, and is associated with the ecstatic trance of the seer.'[53]

Thus it seems that certain aspects of shamanism were kept alive in Europe, including Britain, until the eleventh or twelfth centuries. But what we seem to miss from Odin's shamanism is the positive, healing, integrating, spiritual side. Odin healed only in order to kill again, whereas the true shaman is a saviour, intent on the ultimate spiritual good of both himself and his followers. In this respect we have to see the tendencies of the Germanic and Scandinavian peoples of that time as life-destroying rather than life-enhancing.

ODIN AS RUNE MASTER

Essential to the esoteric side of Odinism is the understanding of the runes, a sacred alphabet. In a famous *Edda* poem, Odin is described as going through an extraordinary process of self-sacrifice in order to gain knowledge of the runes. He is depicted as hanging from the Cosmic Tree, Yggdrasil, impaled by his own spear. There he hung for nine days and nights, a symbolic time associated with the waxing, full and waning moon. The poem reveals Odin as saying:

> Myself given to myself
> On that tree
> Whose roots
> No one knows. . . .
> Into the depths I peered,
> I grasped the runes,
> Screaming I grasped them,
> And then fell back.[118]

'Myself given to myself' might mean the truly mystical understanding of surrender, in which the time-bound psychological self is surrendered to timeless Reality. But it is more likely that Odin was according with the death rites of the time. He, as Lord of Death, had taken himself. He had 'died' in the exact way in which he himself had pronounced that death should take place for all victims – hanging from a tree. This was a common practice in Sweden until the tenth century. Snorri tells us that at the temple of Odin in Uppsala the remains of many victims were to be seen hanging from trees.

Another meaning for the impaling of Odin is his ritual death as a shaman. Through the ceremony of symbolic death, Odin would gain special understanding of the magic of the runes, a secret and hidden knowledge which could only be obtained through the initiation ritual of hanging. The actual pain of the spear might have been the means by which he was 'opened up', the psychic centres of his body pierced. Shamans throughout the world still undertake various painful ordeals, both physical and mental, to aid their practice. It is also likely that the mystery cult of Odin would demand that an initiate should pass certain tests in order to gain Odin's powers – and hanging from a tree might well have been one.

So when the nine days and nights were over, Odin reached down and took the runes. His ordeal was not for the common good but to give himself supreme knowledge. He thus differs fundamentally from Christ, to whom he has sometimes been likened. The contrast between one who sacrifices himself for others, as saviour or saint, and Odin, who wanted to learn the magic of the runes for the power they would give him over others, is a theme which constantly recurs in this chapter.

THE RUNES

The sacred alphabet of the Norse and Saxons is to this day still shrouded in mystery. It is thought that the characters originated in northern Italy and were taken from Stone Age inscriptions carved in rock. The runic characters, with their elongated angular strokes, certainly look as though stone is their natural medium, and it is on stone crosses, standing stones and monuments that we can see them all over Europe to this day.

The word 'rune' is derived from the Indo-European word *ru*, which mean secret or mysterious, and the Old High German word *runer*, which means whisper. Thus the runes were a secret alphabet to be used by practitioners of hidden knowledge – there were charms, sources of occult information, invocations to deities, remedies for pills, runes of war and of grave protection, fertility and birth runes, and weather runes. They were not to be talked about but 'whispered'.[91]

There arose a number of runic alphabets, such as the Germanic, Scandinavian, Old English and Gothic. Occasionally the runes were interspersed with the Celtic alphabet, Ogham. In his book, *The Magic of the Runes*,[91] Michael Howard interprets a number of them, giving the Old English word for each. Thus we get *Beorc*, meaning birch twig. A beating with birch twigs was considered sexually and magically significant; a naked priestess would lie on a bed of birch twigs during fertility ceremonies. *Os* was a god's rune which brought the gift of penetration to divine knowledge. With this rune the user could be in direct touch with Odin (each rune would have had its own sacred ritual, but we have no knowledge of these). *Rad* is a long journey on horseback, the final ride of the hero's soul to Valhalla. *Ken* is a torch, representing the sun and the ritual seasonal fires which were lit to mark its progression through the year on solstice and equinox days. The Scandinavians continued to worship the sun for many centuries. Howard points out that *Ken* is sometimes spelt *Keno*, which is a term used for the ancient fertility goddess Nerthus, whose influence was strong in northern England.

> As we know, the male-dominated solar worship replaced, to some extent, the older, lunar fertility cult of the Great Mother which was widespread in Stone Age Europe. The different spelling and meaning of this rune, and its symbolism, could indicate just how old runic writing really is, for ritual seasonal fires were also a feature of the ancient religion of the Goddess.[90]

Those who cast the runes were regarded as wizards, related by blood to Odin. (Interestingly, most Anglo-Saxon royal houses claimed blood descent from Odin. This claim survived the Anglo-Saxon conversion to Christianity for some time.) The rune-casters were outstanding among the ordinary people because of their dress. They wore a shamanic animal head dress and a deep blue woollen cloak (blue was sacred to Odin). A leather pouch filled with herbs and charms was tied to a girdle, and a staff of ash or hazel carved with runes completed their costume.

Many religions begin with great knowledge and high ideals but gradually decline into superstition. The power of the runes was originally thought to be that of the gods themselves. In India the written name of the deity is still considered to have great potency when meditated upon, for then the attributes of the gods pass into the person. The runes almost certainly started out in this way too. But persecution by the Christian church and also perhaps an innate lack of truth and wisdom within the runes themselves (for the gods were a dangerous lot to invoke) brought about a deterioration in their meaning. Each rune, once intended to convey wisdom, came in the end to be associated with an elemental force or incubus which could be invoked by the right incantations into physical form. Once manifested it had to be very carefully controlled by the rune-master or it could cause untold damage.[25]

Consequently, using the right rune for a situation was of the utmost importance, and Howard recalls the story of Egill, a rune-master, who was asked to cure a dying woman. She had already been prescribed some runes carved on whalebone by a quack rune-master but had not recovered, and Egill soon saw that they were the wrong ones. Angrily he tore them down and placed his own healing runes under her pillow. Within a few minutes she was well again.[90]

Runes continued to be common in Europe until the eleventh and twelfth centuries, and in Iceland until the seventeenth century. They were often used as a secret language to describe the life of Jesus, and the famous Ruthwell Cross at Dumfries is an example of this. The Lord's Prayer, written in runes, was used as a charm. When Christianity succeeded in obliterating runes, they slid underground and were unobtrusively drawn on the back of the hand or cut on the fingernail. Eventually they came to be used as a mason's magical signs and trademarks and were cut into the stonework of some of the great cathedrals and churches.

THOR THE THUNDER GOD

Next in importance to Odin, and only just eclipsed by him, was his eldest son, the great Thunder God Thor, from whom we get Thor's Day, or Thursday. Thor is depicted as a huge figure with a red beard, iron gloves on his hands and wielding a hammer. Of all the Norse gods Thor seems the most characteristic of the stormy, fierce and sometimes over-simple world of the Vikings. He was still worshipped by the Vikings of Dublin until the eleventh century and it was he who was thought by the Christians to be Christ's greatest adversary. It is told that Thor challenged Christ to a single-handed fight, and he was known by Christians as the Black Devil.

Thor was a huge eater and drinker, able to devour a whole ox or two at a sitting, and his enormous gusto for physical living as well as his great strength was shown by the way in which he knocked adversaries out of his path and overcame all obstacles. Never one to be subtle (as Odin was), he merely cracked skulls open with his hammer and when nobody was there he set about shattering the rocks and stones. He killed giantesses with big boulders and felled trees with his hands; by and large he appears to us nowadays as a vast and cheerful oaf with no brain and much liking for a fight. Yet as a god he had enormous influence in Europe. More man-sized images of him were kept in temples than of any other god, and it was always he who was turned to when a difficult decision had to be made.

Thor in his storm-chariot of gold and silver crossing the sky was a common image and it was thought that the rumbling of his chariot caused the sound of thunder. An Icelandic poem gives a vivid picture of Thor, who seems to have been a mixture of Storm and Sun God:

> The Son of Earth drove to the iron game, and the way of the moon resounded before him. . . . The holy places of the powers burned before the kinsman of Ull. Earth, ground of the deep, was beaten with hail as the goats drew the wagon-god for his meeting with Hrungnir. . . . The rocks shook and the boulders were shattered; high heaven burned.[53]

The reference to Hrungnir, the giant (the giants were always the foes of the gods) connects Thor with an esoteric situation.

Hrungnir had inadvertently entered Asgard, the realm of the gods, of which Thor was the chief protector. Thor attacked him with thunder and lightning and hurled his hammer at him. Hrungnir was armed with a whetstone which he flung at Thor. The two weapons collided in mid-air and while the hammer went on to break Hrungnir's head into pieces, the whetstone shattered. One piece shot into Thor's forehead where it lodged – and is said to be there to this day.

The significance of a piece of whetstone in Thor's forehead is that of fire. A whetstone and a hammer together would be the equivalent of a flint and steel to spark a fire. A late saga describes an altar to Thor which was topped with iron, for 'this was the place for the fire which was never allowed to go out. This they call the sacred fire.' Ellis Davidson points out that the connection of Thor with fire seems a genuine one – the Viking Thorolf used fire to claim his land in the name of Thor.[53]

An eternal sacred fire in the forehead of Thor immediately gives a deeper religious dimension to this crude simpleton of a god and perhaps explains why his influence was so great. For through him the lasting fire of illumination might be thought to be apprehended by a devotee, and this fire was also the fire of Thor's lightning. The lightning flash, over which he had supreme power, could also have been the lightning streak of great insight (also known in the Kabbalah) which was transmitted to an initiate. Lightning was considered fire from heaven in many contemporary societies.

The forehead was also thought of by other religions as the seat of enlightenment. In Hinduism it is called the thousand-petalled lotus chakra, where the great flower blooms. If we can accept that Thor was indeed endowed by his believers with the fire of divinity in his head, we can also believe that it was Thor who was referred to in this enigmatic little saying: 'A greater than all – but I dare not even speak his name. And there are few who can see beyond the moment when Odin falls.'[90]

The English worshipped Thor as Thunnor. In a tenth-century charter of Edward the Elder, the title of High Thunderer (Thunnor) was used for the Christian God. Thor's hammer symbol was inscribed on all objects used by society, such as cauldrons and weapons, grave stones and saddles, marriage charters and oaths. With the hammer went the swastika, the prehistoric sign which was particularly adopted by the Norse peoples and became Hitler's insignia. But the hammer, as symbolic of all the battering force of the Norse religion and way of life, was 'not only the symbol of the destructive power of the storm, and of fire from heaven, but also a protection against the forces of evil and violence. Without it Asgard could no longer be guarded against the giants, and men relied on it also to give security and to support the rule of law.'[53]

FREYJA THE GENTLE GODDESS

Such a very blunt and masculine religion hardly seems to have room for a feminine aspect. But, according to Snorri, Freyja was the most beloved of the goddesses and it was she alone who continued to live after the gods were wiped out by Christianity. This implies that her worship was still continuing in the Scandinavia of Snorri's time.

The gentle Freyja who dwelt in Asgard was particularly concerned with human love and fertility – in this she was an Earth Goddess. But she also received the dead, taking half those slain in battle (the other half went to Odin) in her soft arms and comforting them. Her tears – and she shed many – were said to be of gold.

Her greatest attribute, and one which accounts perfectly for the continuation of her worship up to Snorri's time, was that she was a shamaness. She could take on the form of a bird and travel great distances. Snorri linked her with a particular form of shamanism called *seior*, and a certain amount is known from written sources about *seior*. Davidson tells us that a high platform or seat was where the shamaness sat, raised on cushions stuffed with hen's feathers. She was known as a volva, or spae-wife, or seer, and she sang her spells sitting on the platform and working herself up into a state of ecstasy, often accompanied by music and singing from her audience. When she had entered a trance state those present could question her on any personal matter and her answers were thought to come from a different level of consciousness.[53]

Volvas would travel from farm to farm and were invited to all wedding and funeral feasts. A volva could be distinguished by her costume, for in true shamanic tradition it consisted of animal skins. She always wore white gloves made from the skin of cats and boots made of calfskin. Although a volva had the power to do harm, in practice it rarely occurred, and she was welcomed everywhere for her occult seeing and healing powers.

Freyja herself was said to travel in a carriage drawn by cats. It seems that cats were the chosen animal spirits for her shamanic journey and perhaps her tradition has come down the ages in the form of the witch and her familiar, the cat. In her harmful aspect she was said to ride a horse and to crush to death any who had offended her, thus showing that she had a savage side to her nature. But she was a goddess of the Vanir, a rival group of gods to the Aesir, and the women of the Vanir were well known for their malignant ways and also for the cult of the horse. Not only Christians but even the Vikings themselves were sometimes appalled by some of the deeds committed by the followers of the Vanir goddesses.

BALDER THE BEAUTIFUL

The goddess Frigg, who was also of the Vanir, seems to have escaped this split nature. Although not universally loved like Freyja, she was the wife of Odin and mother of his sons and was given unmixed respect everywhere. It was she who protected her beautiful son, the golden Balder, when he was ill with constant nightmares of death. She extracted a promise from all the earth that nothing would harm him. When the promise had been given, the gods would hurl their weapons at him for fun, knowing that he would not be hurt. But the jealous god Loki discovered that Frigg had not included the mistletoe in her promise, for she thought it too young to be harmful. Loki went to an elf smith with a sprig of mistletoe and had it formed into a sharp arrow. Then he persuaded Hoder, Balder's blind brother, to aim his bow at Balder and let fly the fatal arrow. It struck Balder in the heart and he died. For this crime Loki was chained to a rock for all eternity while a poisonous snake perpetually spat scalding venom in his face.

The story of Balder bears some resemblance to the beautiful Greek god Adonis, gashed to death by a boar and forced to live in the underworld. But whereas Adonis was resurrected by decree of Zeus and delivered to the fertility goddess Aphrodite for some of the year (thus re-enacting the seasons), the unfortunate Balder could not be resurrected. Hermod, another son of Odin's, rode off into the underworld of Hel to find him. The goddess Hel agreed to let him return to earth 'if every single creature up in heaven, dead or alive, really mourns him. But he will stay with Hel if only one refuses to mourn him or speaks against him.'[25] All the world agreed to weep for Balder except for one old crone in a cave, an incarnation of Loki, who said she did not care for Balder and would not mourn him. So his resurrection was prevented by one creature filled with hatred and he remained forever in Hel.

Perhaps this story, which shows the eventual triumph of hate over love, typifies the Norse legends which were so full of blood-lust and killing and are in such contrast to the serenity of Greece and Rome and the enchantment of the Celts. A strange and shattering force swept Europe with the advance of first the rapacious Germanic tribes and then the cruel Vikings. It may be that we have not recovered from it yet. In spite of those who admire the devil-may-care bravery of the fighting Norsemen, the impression left with many of us is that of a savage and brutal barbarianism, devoid of higher beliefs such as unconditional love, surrender of the ego, and peaceful harmony with one's neighbour. It seems unlikely that the legends about dragons and underground monsters such as occur in the classic story of Beowulf, or the Frost giants and Mountain Giants who are the enemies of the people and of the gods and also of all that is good, or even the minor elves, trolls and incubuses, could do much to ennoble or enrich mankind. Yet the goings-on of these creatures and of the gods was as much a part of the interest of everyday life in a large part of Europe as the activities of television soap operas are to us today.

WYRD AND THE DOWNFALL OF THE GODS

Hitler made use of the Norse stories for his own ends. It is not clear whether he believed in the power of fate, called Urdr (in Old English, Wyrd). Wyrd was the chief Norn sister who spun the thread and weaved the cloth of the lives of men. In Norse eyes she became omipotent, an all-powerful and inevitable Destiny.

When Christianity was seeking to establish itself, the people became confused between Wyrd and God. They both wielded absolute power over human lives and therefore could not both exist at the same time. As Branston points out, when such a situation occurs one of them must either be effaced or incorporated into the other. In the case of England, Wyrd was for some time the dominant force – 'the glories of Christ are great; Wyrd is the strongest of them all'. But during the eighth to ninth centuries God proved to have the greater attraction and Wyrd's independent power was replaced by a position as an attribute of God – his Providence. King Alfred wrote in 888 AD: 'What we call Wyrd is really the work of God about which He is busy every day.'[25]

As it grew into the accepted religion the Christian church suppressed both the name and idea of Wyrd. But it was not forgotten and both Wyrd and her sisters were kept alive for many centuries, even until Shakespeare's time, when we see them reappear in Macbeth as the 'three weird sisters', able to foretell the future and influence what is about to happen. The notion of Wyrd is perhaps with us still when we touch wood as a tribute to fate to prevent some calamity, for wood means a tree and the Tree of Yggdrasil was the abode of the sisters. Whether for dark or light, many of our customs and the words of our language still reflect the power of the old religion.

With the death of Balder, the reign of the gods was over. It had always been prophesied that a time of doom would come when a great winter of three years would be followed by terrifying earthquakes, the eclipse of the sun and the letting loose of all the monsters from the underworld. The giants would overcome Asgard, and the World Serpent, coiled around the earth, would cause the sea to rise and overwhelm the world.

It is thought that the Mystery cult of Odin was then to be established by the gods to resurrect his spirit so that the earth would grow fair and green again. Perhaps in such mystery practices the Norse were beginning to accept a world where love and resurrection could replace hate and death.

CHAPTER TEN
The Holy Family and the old gods

Christianity began to spread throughout Europe in the second century AD. At first it was one of many cults such as that of Lug, Mithra, Bacchus and others, but by the time the Roman Emperor Constantine was involved with Christianity in the fourth century, there were already a number of small established communities and his great gift to them was that of civil rights. From then on the organisation of the church began to take place, with bishops appointed to major cities.

When Constantine himself was converted to Christianity it became the official Roman religion, perhaps helped by the fact that he continued to identify Christ with Sol Invictus, the Unconquered Sun. But the cult of Sol Invictus was

> essentially a simple cult of the sun, followers of Orpheus, Mithras or Apollo could all find common ground in it. Nor could the Christians grumble. Although in the East there lingered an abhorrence, inspired by the Jews, for representational images, in the West Christians had begun representing Jesus in the guise of the sun god Apollo or Orpheus, the priest of the sun.[174]

To the people of western Europe in those early centuries, Christian ideas were familiar from other sources. Belief in the virgin birth, in the Son who was also the Father, and the god who died and was resurrected, were all well-known themes from the fertility religions. When Easter was established (named after the fertility and light goddess Eostra, and occurring on the date of both the Jewish Passover and the annual resurrection of Adonis), the lament for the death of God's Son on Good Friday, followed by the ceremonies of joy at his resurrection on Easter Sunday – the first day of the sun following the first full moon after the spring equinox – would have seemed natural and proper to a culture still dominated by the seasons. And the ritual of the Eucharist, which bore a strong resemblance to the sacrament of Mithraism, was entirely satisfactory in that it accorded with ancient rites –

> the same Jesus Christ is both the priest and the sacrifice, whose body and blood are truly contained in the sacrament of the altar under the species of bread and wine, the bread being transubstantiated into the body and wine into the blood by the divine power, in order that, to accomplish the mystery of unity, we ourselves may receive of His that which He received of ours.

The eating of the transubstantiated flesh and blood of the deity was a rite which had been practised since Cro-Magnon times and there was nothing strange in believing the physical Christ to be present.

Then too, since the time of Constantine, Christ as a warrior fighting the forces of evil had been the common image, and such an ancient theme accorded with both the belief in him as a Sun God and as a Sky God ('Gentle Jesus, meek and mild' was unknown in early Christianity). In *The Dream of the Rood*, an eighth-century Anglo-Saxon poem, Christ is referred to as 'the young hero' who mounts the Cross as though he were a warrior meeting death in battle.[25]

Nevertheless, in spite of the familiar ideas, there was considerable antagonism to Christianity when it was forced on to the people, with a church built where an older religious sanctuary had stood. 'They have taken away the ancient rites and customs, and how the new ones are to be attended to, nobody knows'[13] was the grumble of the country people. Also it seems that in times of trouble not enough solace was to be found in the Christian religion – 'at a time of plague some had even abandoned the Christian sacraments and had recourse to the delusive remedies of idolatry, as though they could expect to halt a plague ordained by God by spells, amulets, and other devilish secret arts.'[13] But on the whole the people accepted Christianity while still keeping in touch with earlier gods, a state of affairs the church tried hard to stamp out but to little avail. 'The sites of Paganism and Christianity passed one into the other, a mystifying blend that could still be found in this century in the Gaelic phrase commonly in use: "Am bheil thu dol d'on clachan?" It can be translated with equal precision as "Are you going to the stones?" or "Are you going to church?" '[87]

The actual life of Jesus was enlarged on over the centuries and a number of stories were circulated about him, not always complimentary. Some depicted Jesus as a child who showed a malevolent side to his nature by using his supernatural powers to blight or damage as well as to heal. In one story he turned some frightened children who were hiding from him into pigs. In another, when he was making mud pies in a stream, the child who was depriving him of water by damming up the stream was made to drop dead and only when Mary pleaded with him did Jesus bring the child back to life.[89]

Along with such stories there was also a rural, bawdy mirth at the domestic life of Mary and Joseph – particularly the story of Joseph leaving his virgin betrothed to go on a journey and returning to find her pregnant by a ghost. A fifteenth-century play from the Chester Miracle Cycle has Joseph bursting out in resentment:

> . . . Three monethes shee hath bine from me
> Now hasse she gotten her, as I see
> A great belly like to thee
> Syth she went away.[89]

THE QUEEN OF HEAVEN

A hundred years after the Nicene Council of 325 AD, when Jesus was deified and entitled 'very God through all eternity', the position of his mother came under review. There was some effort on the part of the Bishop of Constantinople to maintain that Mary was human and therefore could only have mothered the humanity of Jesus. But the Patriarch Cyril felt she should be divine and at a council packed with his own supporters he got his way. In the year 431 AD it was decreed that she should be known as 'Mother of God' and from then on the cult of Mary thrived, particularly in the Mediterranean countries. She took on many of the characteristics of the archetypal Mother Goddess and was idolised and worshipped in much the same way, with her statuettes to be found in every church. In 1854 all Catholics were asked to accept that from the moment of her conception she was 'kept free from all stain of original sin'. In 1950 Pope Pius XII pronounced that she had been taken up to heaven bodily and was to be known as the 'Queen of Heaven'.

In fact Mary posed a problem for the church for not only was she the Mother of God but she was also the Bride of God who had borne His Son. Only by the uniqueness of Jesus's virgin birth, it was thought, could her immaculate status be sustained. So it was decreed that her virginity was the hope for the salvation of the world. In the early centuries she came to be seen as Eve, and Jesus as the new Adam. The old Adam and Eve had sinned by eating the forbidden apple, and their eyes had then been opened to their carnal nature. The punishment for this 'original sin' had been that all generations from thenceforth would feel carnal desire when procreating children – thus repeating the sin for evermore. But now, through the Virgin-Mother, the Sacred Vessel, Jesus had been stainlessly created by God; and the first state of innocence, or 'original grace', could be seen again in the Son of God who had come down to earth to bring men to a new salvation. Many medieval paintings and artefacts show Mary giving the apple to her son. In his acceptance of the apple from the Sacred Tree, Jesus is the newly created Adam and Mary the stainless Eve. By replaying the original scene, they redeemed it.[89]

Underlying Mary's virgin state was also another factor, the knowledge found throughout the old religious world that virginity was 'powerful magic and conferred strength and ritual purity.[163] In the second century the oriental goddess Cybele was popular in Rome and Europe. She was served by 'vestal virgins' and by eunuchs as part of her mystery cult because of the belief that 'continence is a magic state of power, rather than from ethical considerations about the immorality of sex itself'.[163] Such a belief, which for many centuries had inspired people to abstain from food, drink and sex in order to develop the power to unite with a deity, undoubtedly influenced the Christian celibate priesthood.

Another Mary-event which aroused much discussion, particularly in the Middle Ages, was the mystery of how she became pregnant. Jesus was partly human so there had to be a male involved in his conception. The Gospel writer Luke had described this supplier as the Holy Spirit, or Holy Ghost, but that was not felt to be enough and it was thought essential to know exactly how it all had been managed. Many theologians believed that the Holy Ghost had penetrated Mary's body by way of her right ear and had deposited there either the male element for Jesus's conception or the actual foetus itself. Comparatively little was known about conception and even as late as the twelfth century it was often thought that the whole foetus was implanted into the woman's body by the man, which is why a theologian such as St Thomas Aquinas decided that woman was a mere vessel and had no part to play in procreation.

Decrees made by church authorities needed to be shown in picture form to the largely illiterate people. There are still pictures in existence which show the already formed holy Child sliding down a shaft of light which extends from God into Mary's ear. In the late Middle Ages, statuettes of Mary were made with little doors in her back which, when opened, revealed a small, perfect, removable child.[89]

As Earth Goddess, Mary's popularity was often greater than that of her male Family. With her baby in her arms, she was Fertility itself. To this day she is closer to poor people because of the favours she can bestow – a male child, a good crop, a loving partner, healing for the sick – than the more remote Jesus or God.

During the early centuries the church absorbed the ancient sun and moon beliefs into itself, and Ambrose and Augustine envisaged the sun as Christ and the moon as the church. Later the moon was more naturally associated with Mary and all the church lunar imagery became hers, so that Pope Innocent III could urge the sinful:

> Towards the Moon it is he should look, who is buried in the shades of sin and iniquity. Having lost grace, the day disappears and there is no more sun for him, but the Moon is still on the horizon. Let him address himself to Mary; under her influence thousands every day find their way to God.[163]

As Moon Goddess, Mary was also associated with the sea and its tides, and one interpretation of her name is that it was taken from the Latin for sea, *mar*. The colour of her robes was always blue, that of the sea and sky. Marina Warner tells us that a slip of a copyist's pen turned *stilla maris* (essence of the sea) into *stella maris* (star of the sea) and from then on she appeared as the Pole Star, a guide over the oceans, the lovely image giving rise to a wealth of art and literature: 'If the winds of temptation arise, if you are diving upon the rocks of tribulation, look to the star, invoke Mary.'[163]

The powerful ancient symbol of the serpent, associated with eternal life and wisdom, was also connected with the newborn moon through its ability to slough its skin. But Christianity invested it with loathsomeness and sexual connotations (perhaps because of the moon's links with menstruation). Mary is often depicted trampling on the serpent. Yet 'although its presence in images of the Immaculate Conception is negative, it continues to form with the moon and the stars and the waters an elaborate code of the mysteries of life, growth, and birth over which the woman – the Virgin Mary – is believed to hold sway.'[163] Thus (as in much of Christian symbolism) there is an inherent contradiction in the act of the Virgin treading beneath her feet the symbol of carnality while she is at the same time worshipped as the goddess of human, animal and vegetable fertility.[163]

No better way of describing her true influence as Earth Goddess can be found than this twelfth-century prayer dedicated to her, which comes from an English herbal:

> Earth, divine goddess, Mother Nature, who dost generate all things and bringest forth ever anew the sun which thou hast given to the nations; Guardian of sky and sea and of all Gods and powers; through thy influence all nature is hushed and sinks to sleep. . . . Thou indeed art rightly named Great Mother of the Gods; Victory is in thy divine name. Thou art the source of the strength of peoples and gods; without thee nothing can either be born or made perfect; thou art mighty, Queen of the Gods.[53]

THE SAINTS

Worship of the saints turned Christianity into a comfortably polytheistic religion for most people. When Jesus or Mary failed, succour might still be found from a local saint. And support was badly needed. Plagues swept over Europe, decimating the population. There was a strong division between rich and poor, and the poor were very poor – although usually saved from starvation by lord or monastery. Many were slaves; and the church made no move to abolish slavery. For those who could earn a living from their own land, there were crippling tithes to be paid to church and country. But in most communities there lived or had lived a holy man or woman to whom the people could turn in their troubles, and a number of stories are told of saints intervening to prevent harsh treatment of slaves.

As well as the famous saints there were many minor ones, such as St Wita of Whitchurch Canonicorum in Dorset. It is thought she was a holy hermit who was put to death for her faith in 831 when hundreds of Vikings landed on the coast four miles away. Fifty years later Alfred the Great, who took much interest in those martyred for their faith, built a church called St Wita's on the spot where the present church now stands, and it is thought that this replaced the hermitage where her relics had been preserved. Her shrine has been kept intact to this day. A lead casket containing her bones (recently verified) lies on a stone stand. Into the stone are cut 'limb holes' where a sufferer could thrust an injured arm or leg for closer contact with the saint. She was believed to be a healer of the sick and even today many written pleas for healing are pushed through the limb holes. For centuries her shrine was a place of pilgrimage. In this exceptionally beautiful part of England, where woods and hills still retain ancient trackways, an aura of peace and calm envelopes the small old church, affecting even the most sceptical, and who is to say that its source is not the coffin of a woman of healing and luminous vision.

A saint famous throughout Europe was Michael, the archangel. In the Old Testament he is called 'the captain of the heavenly host' who won victory during 'a war in heaven'.[17] He was honoured in the west as a protector of Christians and especially of soldiers. Many scholars believe that he was confused in popular religion with the Celtic sky-god Lug, for churches dedicated to Michael were usually built (most often on the sites of more ancient shrines) on the tops of hills and rocky crags, as though to attract him in his flight – such as Mont St Michel, St Michael's Mount, the Church of Michael de Rupe in Dartmoor, and the Chapel of Saint Michael at Le Puy en Velay. Prayers to Michael ring with imagery of battle:

Thou Michael the victorious,
I make my circuit under thy shield,
Thou Michael of the white steed,
And of the brilliant blades,
Conqueror of the dragon,
Be thou at my back,
Thou ranger of the heavens,
Thou warrior of the King of all. . . .[38]

It has been noted that the Welsh word *tan*, which means fire, used to mean a beacon fire on a hill top in Celtic times. Santan was a Celtic Fire God and his name in Christian times became St Anne. Many hills, when not crowned by a church to St Michael, are called St Anne's Hill in memory of those beacon fires.

During the first thousand years of Christianity the church was not sufficiently established to stamp out the practices of other religions completely – the great persecutions were still to follow in the Middle Ages. Indeed, when Augustine first came to Britain in 597, a much greater spirit of toleration existed, partly due to the strong Pope Gregory, than was to be seen again for a long time. Perhaps it was because the doctrine of the Church was still imbued with the spirit of the early Christians and it did not feel it had to affirm itself by denying others. The way (including the king's bribe) by which Christianity came to be accepted in Britain is touchingly told by Bede:

> As soon as they had occupied the house given to them they began to emulate the life of the apostles and the primitive Church. They were constantly at prayer; they fasted and kept vigils; they preached the word of life to whomsoever they could. They regarded worldly things as of little importance, and accepted only the necessities of life from those they taught. They practised what they preached; and were willing to endure any hardship, and even to die for the truth which they proclaimed. Before long a number of heathen, admiring the simplicity of their holy lives and the comfort of their heavenly message, believed and were baptised.[13]

WOMEN AND THE OLD RELIGION

However much the family of God was accepted by western Europeans, they nevertheless still longed for celebrations of the seasons and for contact with Goddess Earth and Moon through the old fertility rituals. As far as possible the Church took over the festivals of the seasons and gave them Christian names, usually those of the saints or holy personages. For instance, it was decreed in the fourth century that the birth of Christ was to be celebrated on 25 December, the winter solstice festival kept in most countries;

and the association of Jesus with a sun god (Sol Invictus) fixed his weekly holy day as Sun-Day, rather than its original Saturn (cold and wet) Day, or Saturday. Such activities as fertility rites were forbidden, however, for the people should be directing their thoughts to heaven and not to earth.

Also frowned on was the role of women in any rituals. Gone were the days when Celtic women were equal to their men and druidesses stood beside druids in battle. With the abhorrence of sex which developed in Christianity (inherited from Judaism which, like the other desert religion of Zoroastrianism, saw women as degraded beings; and enhanced by St Paul) the place of women in society plummeted down. The wise Pope Gregory of the early seventh century instructed Augustine that women should be allowed inside a church during menstruation and after childbirth, thus overturning rules which the Old Testament had firmly laid down (that, for instance, a woman could not enter a church until her newborn son was thirty-three days old or daughter sixty-six days old), but he was exceptional for his fair-mindedness.[13]

And even Pope Gregory could not conceive of women as the equal of men in spiritual matters. Hence those women who stood out in their community as having psychic gifts or a natural understanding of plants and animals were frowned on by the church and practised their talents unobtrusively. They were the interpreters of the old belief that the whole of nature was divine, every entity an interconnecting and vital force. Margaret Murray has shown that this ancient cult was a second religion throughout Europe, with even Christian priests and bishops occasionally performing in its rites.[125] For at that time most communities were agricultural and a God who took no interest in the fertility of the land and of animals was no use to men – hence a code of morality came a great deal second-best to a fertility ceremony which could fill an empty belly.

Pope Gregory recognised this feeling and instructed Augustine that if he found beliefs among the pagans which were so deeply rooted that they could not easily be removed, they were to be turned into Christian practices,

> and since they have a custom of sacrificing many oxen to demons, let some other solemnity be substituted in its place, such as a day of Dedication or the Festivals of the holy

> martyrs. . . . On such occasions they might well construct shelters of boughs for themselves around the churches that were once temples, and celebrate the solemnity with devout feasting. They are no longer to sacrifice beasts to the Devil, but they may kill them for food to the praise of God, and give thanks to the Giver of all gifts for the plenty they enjoy.[13]

If the advice of Gregory had continued to be carried out there would have been no blood and bitterness to be laid at the door of the church.

Witches and their persecutions were to come later, but their covens were based on the knowledge passed down the centuries by the women of the 'older' religion of the shamans – knowledge of the Moon Goddess and her powers, the rites of fertility, and of sacred herbs and potions; knowledge which honoured Mother Earth and believed in the great rhythms of the energies of life.

THE HORNED ONE

Many of the Celtic gods and goddesses were absorbed into Christianity, such as Michael and Bridget of Ireland and a host of others. Dragon-slaying gods became St George and storm gods St Elias. There was one who was never absorbed, however, and who came to be looked upon as a 'horned devil' by the Christians – the god Cernunnos. In Britain and Celtic France he was believed to have a particular affinity with stags and to possess supernatural powers over them. Worship of this forest deity continued well into the Middle Ages, probably in secret glades, and we can see frequent reminders of him carved in churches and portrayed in annual festivals. The Green Man or Wild Man can be seen in a church such as Sampford Courtenay in Somerset, where the smiling head is surrounded by leaves, while roots emerge from his mouth. A man covered in green branches is the central figure of many springtime festivals throughout Europe. He is known as Jack in the Green (or in the Bush), Robin of the Wood, May Man, or King of the May, and he probably embodies the green energy of trees as well as representing the creative force of the tree spirit bringing back new life after the winter death. Dancing round trees seems to have been an essential part of tree-worship and there were special 'dancing trees' in Devon round which it took place at certain times of the year. Such circle dances (in some a ring is formed with 'Robin Goodfellow' in the middle) can be traced back 30,000 years, for in a Spanish cave there is a carved circle of women dancing who all have peaked hoods, long breasts and long hair.

The carved wild men of churches frequently wear horns and their origin is Cernunnos. The stag dance performed to this day at Abbot's Bromley is a celebration of a much older version. The remarkable Horned Mask of the Dorset Ooser (recently stolen) shows the need people continued to have for contact with the supernatural animal world. The church, of course, strongly opposed any celebration of this sort: 'If anyone at the kalends of January goes about as a stag or a bull; that is, making himself into a wild animal and dressing in the skin of a herd animal, and putting on the heads of beasts; those who in such wise transform themselves into the appearance of a wild animal, penance of three years, because this is devilish.'[13]

Nikolai Tolstoy connects the Horned God with Merlin the magician. Merlin is represented in early Welsh poetry as having an unusual mastery over stags. When his wife was about to marry another, Merlin brought together a herd of deer and, himself mounted on a stag, led the herd to the wedding. When he saw the bridgegroom he tore off the horns he was wearing and hurled them at the man, smashing his head in. He then rode back to the forests.[158]

Merlin was undoubtedly identified with an animal deity. He was said to live an animal existence as one of the herd, eating as they ate, roots, grasses, wild fruits and berries. He seems to have been physically like a stag but with a man's nature and it is possible that the Greek god Pan, who was half man and half animal, with hooves and horns, had something to do with the legend. For Pan was known throughout Europe as the god of the forests. Tolstoy makes the point that the birth resemblance is similar too: 'At Pan's birth . . . when the nurse saw his uncouth face and full beard, she was afraid and sprang up and left the child', just as the women attending Merlin's birth were disquieted by the appearance of his hairy pelt, 'such as they had never seen on another child'.[158]

But Merlin was not merely a Wild Man of the forests, he was also a shaman. And there is plenty of evidence to show that 'the original Merlin saga comprised the story of a late British shaman-figure' –

in Tolstoy's view a real person who lived and died in southern Scotland. Geoffrey of Monmouth, whose twelfth-century account of King Arthur and Merlin fuelled a fire of speculation about the magic of these islands which is burning still, described Merlin as becoming 'mad' in just the way a shaman feels the 'call' to prepare for his journey:

> He threw dust upon his hair, tore his clothes and lay prostrate on the ground, rolling to and fro. . . . Then, when the air was full with these repeated loud complainings, a strange madness came upon him. He crept away and fled to the woods, unwilling that any should see his going. Into the forest he went, glad to lie hidden beneath the ash trees. . . . [69]

His identification with a stag would have meant that he moved like a stag, called like them and became in himself a projection of the animal deity, as in the old shamanic practices. It is not hard to imagine the influence such a figure would have had in early Christian Britain (and he had equivalents in Ireland and elsewhere) nor how detestable the Christians would have found him. Nor is it difficult to see how he merged into and later became the Horned God of the witches, a fertility figure who was worshipped at special feasts where he was the consort of Diana the Moon Goddess, and whose body, blood and soul were consumed in bread and wine.

It was in the Middle Ages that the Holy Grail romances were written and the spell of the Round Table of King Arthur and his Knights brought back the old Celtic tales and their characters such as Merlin. What is revealed of Merlin there rings with an authority derived from earlier centuries: 'I was taken out of my true self, I was as a spirit and knew the history of people long past and could foretell the future. I knew then the secrets of nature, bird flight, star wanderings and the way fish glide.'[158]

Tolstoy believes that the ever-present legend of the heavenly god Lug and the story of Merlin merged: 'He is Lug, the brightness which brings dawning self-awareness, culture and the approximation of man to God. And ultimately he dies the sacrificial death of Lug, the ultimate self-sacrifice of god who suffers vicariously, redeeming the plight of man created in His image.'[158]

KING ARTHUR AND THE HOLY GRAIL

In recent times the documents relating to King Arthur have been scrutinised with scientific precision. It is now believed that the Arthur who appears in the Latin narratives of Celtic Britons was a real man. The earliest documents refer to him as the leader of Britons who mounted a series of battles against the Saxons at the end of the fifth century. It is now thought that this was so and that he died in battle at the beginning of the sixth century.

How, then, did the famous legends of the sword in the stone, the court of Camelot, the Knights of the Round Table and the quest for the Holy Grail, come to be attached to a rather shadowy British chieftain whose life was spent in battle? First we should look at the sources for our knowledge. As well as the Latin accounts there are Welsh traditional stories, written in Welsh, which give Arthur unfamiliar roles, such as leading a raid on the 'otherworld'. These can be found in the Welsh classic, the Mabinogi.[110] Then there is a group of medieval French stories based on spoken Celtic sources, and it is they who introduce us to the traditional Camelot, Round Table and quest for the Grail. As well, they tell us of Lancelot, who is not mentioned in the Mabinogi.[69]

Through the writings of Geoffrey of Monmouth in the twelfth century, Chrétien de Troyes[44] of France also in the twelfth century, and Malory of France in the fifteenth century, the court of King Arthur came to life. It was associated with amazing and supernatural happenings so that until quite recently Arthur was regarded as a fantasy figure and was never referred to in history books. Now that it is known that he was a real person, the task of historians is to understand how the French Celtic stories in particular (because they are the most descriptive) came into being. It is now accepted that all the Athurian legend is myth or romance and that even Camelot is an invention of the French medieval poets, but this does not explain why such a myth should attach itself to Arthur.

The scholar John Darrah has suggested that Arthur, 'like many another personage important in oral "literature" has attracted into orbit round himself material which does not belong to his period at all'.[52] This does not quite answer the question but Francis Hitching has a theory which perhaps does:

> In the millennia during which the stone circles were being built, Polaris and its constellation the Great Bear were steadily moving towards the North Pole in place of two stars contained in the constellation Draco (the Dragon). In Welsh, and phonetically in Celtic, the Great Bear is Arth Vawr. Scattered over Great Britain and Ireland are more than 100 sites with the almost indistinguishable name 'Arthur', many of them megalithic sites such as Arthur's Stone, Arthur's Seat, Arthur's Quoit, and so on. The great majority of the latter lie within a north-south aligned scemb line.
>
> In the connection between these ancient megaliths and the pole star may hide the origins of the Arthurian legends. Scholars have always been puzzled why such a huge amount of early medieval literature – some estimates put it as high as one-quarter of the total – are devoted to Arthur; . . . it is difficult to see why European clerics should have been so fascinated with him. If, however, they were writing about a supremely important prehistoric god of the pole star, whose powers were at one time essential to the workings of pagan religion and were then fancifully Christianised, it would fit in with the general pattern whereby the old pagan gods and beliefs were transformed and assimilated into the traditions of the Church.[87]

There is no doubt that Celtic beliefs came to be associated with Arthur and it was from them that the Arthurian legend as we know it was extracted. Many Celtic themes occur in the Arthurian stories such as the severed head found in a well, prediction and foreknowledge, shape-shifting, and the importance of wells and lakes. For instance, in Chrétien de Troyes' Lancelot, 'Gawain crosses a bridge under the water to reach the fortress of Meleagant. This underwater place is very much of the Other World, a kind of Grail Castle with its own Maiden of the Grail. The Welsh legend of Lake Tegid makes her Keridwen, a sorceress-cum-goddess who owns the cauldron of knowledge, and who casts her son Taliesin on the waves in a leather bag after his birth'.[115] This interweaving of Celtic myth with Arthurian legend makes it likely that the Irish god Bran was associated with Arthur too and that Arthur was his legendary successor, taking on many of his magical characteristics.

Geoffrey of Monmouth told the tale that Merlin the Magician

fetched the Stonehenge megaliths from Ireland and placed them in position. Commenting on this story, the historian Stuart Piggott says,

> we may have the only fragment left to us of a native Bronze Age literature – a literature which would be as natural an outcome of a heroic culture such as the Wessex Bronze Age (or that of Mycenae, with which indeed it traded), as are the gold-hilted daggers of the warriors, but so infinitely more perishable. We may have the story of the builder, and of the building of the great monument to the spiritual and political ascendancy of Bronze Age Wessex, handed down as part of the sacred lore of its priests long enough to ensure its incorporation in the legends accumulating round another Wessex leader, a Roman of the Dark Ages; then preserved in the myths of the Celtic west and finally entering the body of written record of the Middle Ages among the legendary miscellanea of a romantic medieval ecclesiastic who may have fancied it as a fairy-tale.[136]

In such a book as this one it may be asked what the religious importance of the Arthurian legend was and still is. The answer is that in the eyes of many it is certainly not just a fairy-tale but represents a secret teaching, a western mystery cult, just as attractive as any of the Greek or Asiatic ones. For the mysteries 'were institutes erected for the transmutation of base ignorance into precious illumination'.[81] The Grail, for instance, in its form as the cup in which drops of Christ's blood were caught at the Crucifixion (its actual form can never be seen by human eyes), is the chalice of immortality; and the Fisher King of the Grail is associated both with the fisherman, a mystery symbol of Christianity, and with the vine – and through wine with the Dionysian cult. The Celtic way of associating one group of symbols with another so that in the end a many-stranded web was produced is characteristic of the Arthurian tales.

Taken as a secret religious teaching, the Arthurian legends embody all the initiatory experiences and symbols of a true mystery cult. The Round Table signifies the universe and all its powers; the Grail is the heart of man – 'the alchemical crucible of evolutionary experience, insofar as its great mystery pertains to human dimensions';[99] the names of the knights and ladies hold vibrations of ancient magical powers. And too, many people read into the legend the Tree of Life of the Jewish Kabbalah.

A deeper knowledge of the symbols takes us into the heart of the mystery cult:

> A knowledge of the implications of the Table Round . . . implies an understanding of cosmic centres of influence working in conjunction with the great spiritual being behind the Sun, and in particular of the type of force focused through contemplation of the stars of Ursa Major.
>
> These stars might be said to express themselves in human terms as the symbolism of the Table Round and the ideals of the Fellowship of the Knights dedicated to a code of conduct. In its broadest sense the Round Table Fellowship is a formula that applies to each human being who has reached a particular level of evolutionary development.
>
> The Grail implies the various powers which come to the human soul as it develops as an individual and as an integral part of the great Divine Pattern.
>
> The Knights and their Ladies, who form the Fellowship, are archetypes of different sorts of force as expressed through human experience, and at the same time each one of them, as a particular type of force, is present within us all.[99]

Such is the language of the authentic mystery cult and it may prove to be of great help to those who need to visualise and imagine their way to that which transcends the imagination. It reveals by its symbols truths of the path and noble aspirations. Some of the eastern forms of religion which have become popular in the west, such as Tibetan Buddhism and Hinduism, use the same principles to help their pupils.

CHAPTER ELEVEN
Hermits and mystics

Whole libraries have been written about the schisms which afflicted the western church in the early centuries. The doctrinal differences were mostly in the heads of theologians and had little connection with the daily life of ordinary people. Nevertheless a subtle and pervasive atmosphere of a new order of things began to spread through western culture. The sense of being part of a divine world gave way to a feeling of estrangement:

> Within a world that is itself divine, where God is immanent throughout, in the impulse of the flight of birds, the lightning, the falling rain, the fire of the sun, there is an epiphany of divinity in all sight, all thought, and all deeds, which – for those who recognise it – is a beginning and end in itself. There is for all, and with all, a universal revelation. Whereas within a world that is not itself divine, but whose Creator is apart, the godhead is made known only by special revelation – as on Sinai, or in Christ, or in the words of the Koran; and righteousness then consists in placing oneself in accord not with nature but with Sinai, with the lesson of Christ or with the Koran; and one lives not simply to play the part well that is in itself the end, like the grapevine producing grapes, but, as Christ has said, 'so that my Father may reward.' The goal is not here and now, but somewhere else.[34]

Among the Celtic peoples of the west, however, the feeling of harmony with the universe was never quite lost. This was partly because the Roman influence did not extend to western fringes such as Ireland and Brittany, and until the seventh century the Pope was not acknowledged by the Celts. But mainly it was because the people themselves were not akin to a legalistic state Christianity, which was the pattern of the Roman Church, and were far closer to the majesty and mysteries of the universe than to a formalised set of doctrines.

But the teaching of Christianity itself was welcomed gladly. The miracle stories were food and drink to the Celts, for their own mythology was also filled with strange happenings. They delighted in the wonders and found no difficulty in accepting Christ as a god with unusual powers, similar to those the druids had possessed. And the fact that Christianity thought in threes – the Holy Trinity, the Holy Family, the rising of Christ after three days, his crucifixion at the third hour, the fact that he was one of three victims, that darkness fell upon the land at the sixth hour and he died at the ninth hour – all this made it pleasantly familiar to the Celts who themselves had always thought in threes (as did the Egyptian cult of Isis). 'The little drop of the Three' came to be the baptismal Christian drop on the forehead to protect against 'fays', gnomes and spectres.'[38] As well, to belong to the family of God was a great sign of status, particularly among the Irish who were very concerned with their ancestry.

But deeper than this was a feeling of joy in the nobility of the new religion. For the Christianity which travelled to Brittany and Ireland was that of the monastic and ascetic life. By way of travelling monks news reached the far west of the Desert Fathers, the hermits who peopled the caves of Egypt, Arabia and Palestine in the fourth century. The Fathers were men who believed that Christianity was a spiritual state of being. They also believed, as did Jesus, that all people should be equal in society, with God as the supreme authority. And, most important, they 'sought a way to God that was uncharted and freely chosen, not inherited from others who had mapped it out beforehand. They sought a God whom they alone could find, not one who was "given" in a set, stereotyped form by somebody else.'[120]

THE WANDERING HERMITS

Such a spirit was eagerly greeted by the Celts, always great individualists. The example of the Desert Fathers set men journeying far distances in search of places where they could be alone to pray and contemplate. A longing for solitude had always been an inherent part of the Celtic temperament and from the fifth to the ninth centuries the west was full of wandering monks 'listening' to the voice of God, and seeking the 'Land of Promise' where a cell might be built and wisdom won in silence and meditation. To the Hebrides and Orkneys they went, to lonely islands in English lakes and in the Atlantic off the coasts of Wales and Brittany. Love of the sound of water and of water birds, the sighing of the wind, and the seeing of the green land about them kept them close to the cosmic mystery of existence and far from the Roman church.

> It is for this I love Derry,
> For its smoothness, for its purity;
> All full of angels
> Is every leaf on the oaks of Derry.[56]

They believed that the presence of God could be experienced in the moment and not in some future time. 'God is near to all who call upon Him'[93] said a woman saint. They lived lives of the utmost austerity and a tenth-century writer reported, 'they have need of nothing but to be listening to the music to which they listen, and to look on the light which they see and to be filled with the fragrance which is in the land.'[93]

In the simplicity of their lives, animals, birds and fish played as magical a role as they had in the mythological past. When St Brendan was singing Mass in his boat he was surrounded by porpoises who leapt in delight and then swam away when Mass was over. St Claran's first follower was a boar who built him a cell of twigs and grass torn up by his tusks; he was soon joined by a fox, a wolf and a badger. The hermit Paul was served by a sea-otter who brought him fish and firewood. A stag held a book open on his antlers for St Cainneck to read, and a bird dropped a feather for St Molaisse to make into a pen when he wanted to write a book.[93]

After long wrangling over the proper date for Easter, the Celtic and Roman churches eventually began to come together in the seventh century. But it was not until the fierce Viking invasions that the way of the wandering hermit-saint was brought to an end. With its passing went much that was attractive and noble in western Christianity.

THE CHRISTIAN MYSTICS

The Celts were not alone in their longing for oneness with the Godhead. In the Roman Church too there were great mystics who followed a path closer to the old Greek thought than to the new western Christianity. They longed to 'know' in the deepest, fullest, closest sense possible the Supreme Reality of their lives. In their quest for such a fulfilment they were prepared to give up everything; for the mysterious and wonderful wholeness which they sought seemed to heal the sense of separation and incompleteness intrinsic to their humanness. 'I am sure,' said Eckhart, a later mystic who was accused of heresy, 'that if a soul knew the very least of all that being means, it would never turn away from it.'[161] The mystics felt God to be immanent in all existence, the Essence and Ground of it, and not remote from it as in doctrinal Christianity. They saw the world as the 'self-revelation of the in-dwelling Deity'.[161] It was not a static world projected from an outside 'Maker', but rather a dynamic World of Becoming, creating itself, filled with the spirit of the Godhead in which every atom of the universe partook equally. Eckhart said, 'God is nearer to me than I am to myself; He is just as near to wood and stone but they do not know it.'[9]

Their mysticism was greatly inspired by the Greek writer Plotinus for whom union with the Absolute was the highest goal. His insights and language were to have a lasting effect on mystical Christianity. He believed in a triad. First there was the Source, the essential principle of life which, like the Tao, contained all and was all. To know the Source and to be at one with it was the ultimate reason for existence. Plotinus was said to be 'ever tending towards the Divine which he loved with all his heart'.[161]

Below the Source but emanating from it was the Mind, the world of ideas and thought-forms. This was the realm of meaning – where understanding has its place and all concepts coexist in a timeless Now.

And thirdly was the World Soul, the creative energy which harmonised the timeless Now world with time and space and the physical universe. From the World Soul flowed forth the individual souls which animated bodies. Thus there was no gap between the human individual and the Source itself, for they were one in identity. Through the 'chain of becoming' the individual derived his existence from the Source and was part (though not the whole) of it. The human, said Plotinus, 'belongs to God and is one with him, like two concentric circles; they are one when they coincide; and two only when they are separated'.[9]

The way back to the Source, the spiritual journey of homecoming, was through purification of the senses and detachment from the world. Then the great love for the Divine which lies dormant in every soul would be activated, and identity with the Source rediscovered. Plotinus called this journey 'the flight of the alone to the Alone':

> He who has seen it knows whereof I speak: that the soul has another life as it nears to God, and is now come to him, and has a share in him so that, restored, it knows . . . it needs naught else; and on the other hand we must put aside everything else and abide in This alone, and become This alone – detached from all temporal things . . . no part of the soul not touching God. Then it will be possible for the soul to see both God and herself divinely and . . . she will be light itself – pure, unfettered, agile, become a God or rather being a God, and wholly aflame.[161]

THE DIVINE DARK

In the sixth century the written works of another mystic, Dionysius, began to spread throughout Christendom, and with Plotinus he shares in the creation of the Christian mysticism which later was to burst into flower in the Middle Ages. It affected those Christians whose minds were open and aware, and who longed to be 'oned' with the Ground of their Being. For such seekers, although they paid much lip service to him, the historical figure of Jesus was largely irrelevant – and indeed some of the mystics' own writings seem to be of a deeper nature than the sayings of Jesus himself. Nor was the divinity of Jesus as Christ the Mediator essential, for the journey of the spirit was of the individual directly to the Source. This was not the Christianity of the ordinary people, for whom a life based on the person of Jesus was the goal. Hence there has always existed an uneasy tension in the west between mystics and churchgoers. For Christianity is the only world religion which bases itself on the historical life of an incarnate deity. In all other religions the deity has said 'I point the way' and has pointed beyond himself. But in Christianity Jesus said 'I am the way' and his flocks have believed that his life on earth was what was meant by that statement.

Dionysius was a spiritual follower of Plotinus. In fact it is not known who he really was at all, for the pseudonym he took – Dionysius the Areopagite – was that of a friend of St Paul's. For many centuries it was believed that his writings were indeed those of the original Areopagite. But quotations found in his work have proved that he wrote between 475 and 525 and it is now believed that he was a Syrian monk, perhaps one of the Desert Fathers. In the ninth century his booklet on mystical theology was translated into Latin by John Scotus Erigena and from then to the seventeenth century his writings nourished the greatest spiritual intuitions of Christians and were endowed with enormous authority.

> He kindled in multitudes of souls a pure passion for God, and taught . . . that the one thing worth seeking with the entire being is God. . . . He insisted on personal experience as the primary thing in religion, and so became the father of a great family of devout and saintly mystics. And he maintained 'that there is an experience of Reality which transcends mere head-knowledge – a finding of God in which the whole being, heart, will and mind, are expanded and satisfied, even though language cannot formulate what is being experienced.'[95]

Dionysius was the first Christian writer to describe with accuracy the ways in which a consciousness of the Source worked and how unity with it could be attained. Authoritative advice on how to actually set about the spiritual quest could be found in other religions but was singularly lacking in Christianity where the emulation of Jesus was thought to be the only path. So clear was Dionysius that later contemplatives found their most numenous and sublime experiences described and partly explained by him. When they themselves (Eckhart, Jan of Ruysbroeck, the author of *The Cloud of Unknowing*, St John of the Cross) came to write of their own experiences, they borrowed his language. Hence Christian mysticism resounds with wonderful concepts. The Absolute Godhead is described as 'the Unconditioned', 'the Divine Dark', and 'the negation of all that is'. The way of the soul is by negation, or emptiness, by letting go of all ideas and beliefs, by a 'divine ignorance' – for the Unconditioned is beyond thought since thought can only deal with what is relative and differentiated. Hindus, Buddhists and classical Greek thinkers recognise the terminology but many Christians were, and are still, repelled by it.

Although the Godhead was beyond knowledge, yet it could be reached and experienced; and a loving intensity and submission of will was inherent to this act. Response to the call of the Absolute was that of an action so deep that it involved a turning around in life, a total change of direction. 'Divine love,' says Dionysius, 'draws those whom it seizes beyond themselves: and this so greatly that they belong no longer to themselves but wholly to the Object loved.'[161]

The essence of Dionysius' message is that each of us has to undertake the work of a sculptor on ourselves – 'those who make a statue from the rough stone first remove all the superfluous matter hindering the pure vision of the hidden form and thus reveal the hidden beauty merely by this removal.'[9] The 'hidden beauty', the Godhead, is always there but we who are 'attached to the objects of human thought, and who believe that there is no superessential Reality beyond' blind ourselves to it. We need to free ourselves from our dependencies and by this very act the Godhead will be revealed. Our tool is contemplation, known nowadays as meditation. In one of his most beautiful passages, Dionysius describes how meditation draws the soul towards the oneness it craves

> as if a luminous chain were suspended from the celestial heights, and we, by ever clutching this, first with one hand and then with the other, seem to draw it down, but in reality we are ourselves carried upwards to the high splendours of the luminous rays. Or as if, after we have embarked on a ship and are holding on to the cable reaching to some rock, we do not draw the rock to us, but draw, in fact, ourselves and the ship to the rock.[95]

Dionysius was the first to set out the qualities which affirm God – Good, Being, Life, Wisdom, Power – and to point out how limited such descriptions are and how necessary it is to move beyond them.

> For the higher we soar in contemplation the more limited become our expressions of that which is purely intelligible; even as now, when plunging into the Darkness which is above the intellect, we pass not merely into brevity of speech, but even into absolute silence, of thought as well as of words. At last, the 'entire ascent being accomplished' we become wholly voiceless, inasmuch as we are absorbed in Him who is totally ineffable.[95]

Dionysius' prayer became that of every mystic in the church: 'We pray that we may come into this Darkness which is beyond light, and, without seeing and without knowing, to see and to know that which is above vision and knowledge through the realisation that by not-seeing and by unknowing we attain to true vision and knowledge.'[95]

THE LUMINOUS EVERYDAY WORLD

Many people believe that such insights represent the highest reaches of the human spirit – a level to which we have progressed over the course of millennia, during which time civilisation has become greater and finer. But at the end of a book such as this, another suggestion may be considered. There seem to be three essential beliefs which have upheld humankind since its beginning. These are: that the beingness of oneself is also that of timeless Reality; that to find this basic beingness we have to let go of our dependence on conditioned things; and that when we actually do this, the nature of our true life as a human being is revealed to us – we take up a place of meaning and usefulness in the universe. These intrinsic beliefs have been reflected in all the religions we know about – in their literature and painting, their music and the sayings of their prophets and sages.

Because of the practice of writing we can trace knowledge of the religions back with certainty for at least 6,000 years. Philosophies which are written down seem more right, more valid to us – even though words are often inadequate – than the many religious ideas which preceded writing. But we should not doubt that early man also had his Platos and his Buddhas. Scholars now believe in fact that 'primitive' man may have been much closer to the Ground of his being than we, with all our clever acquisitiveness, are today. Technical progress is often confused with mental and spiritual development, so that many people fail to recognise the full capacity for feeling and understanding in early man.

Therefore I would like to suggest that the true arena is the everyday secular world, the world of light and shadow which is permeated with the numinous and the spiritual and always was. Religion may cordon off areas of this great and miraculous arena, setting up churches and providing rituals for the expression of the sacred. But such rituals in the end fail to hide the truth that 'the sacred is also present in the everyday familiar secular world. It is present most of all because the world is populated by the people, who are sacred, by nature.'[64] As they always were and always will be.

For whatever the historical scene, whatever the conditioning background to their lives, men and women can always sense that there is a greater reality which transcends this world but which is also immanent within it, sanctifying it and making it real. And they are aware that their life is sacred in origin and that they will be able to realise its full potential in so far as they participate in that luminous reality.

Bibliography

(1) Adler, M. (1979), *Drawing Down the Moon*, Boston, Beacon Press.
(2) Allegro, J. (1977), *Lost Gods*, London, Michael Joseph.
(3) Altizer, T.J.J. (1963), *Mircea Eliade and the Dialectic of the Sacred*, Philadelphia, University Press.
(4) Anderson, W. (1983), *Holy Places of the British Isles*, London, Ebury Press.
(5) Atkinson, R.J.C. (1960), *Stonehenge*, Harmondsworth, Penguin.
(6) Attwater, D. (1965), *The Penguin Dictionary of Saints*, Harmondsworth, Penguin.
(7) Auel, J. (1980), *The Clan of the Cave Bear*, London, Hodder & Stoughton.
(8) Bachofen, J.J. (1967), *Myth, Religion and Mother Right*, Princeton, New Jersey, Princeton University Press.
(9) Bancroft, A. (1974), *Religions of the East*, London, Heinemann.
(10) Bancroft, A. (1978), *Modern Mystics and Sages*, London, Granada.
(11) Bancroft, A., (1979), *Zen: Direct Pointing to Reality*, London, Thames & Hudson.
(12) Bancroft, A. (1982), *The Luminous Vision: Six Medieval Mystics*, London, Allen & Unwin.
(13) Bede (1955), *A History of the English Church and People*, trans. L. Sherley-Price, Harmondsworth, Penguin.
(14) Bégouën, M (1925), *The Clay Bisons*, London, Longman.
(15) *Beowulf* (1981), trans. Michael Alexander, Harmondsworth, Penguin.
(16) Berlin, S. (1978), *Amergin, An Enigma of the Forest*, Devon, David & Charles.
(17) Bianchi, U. (1975), *The History of Religions*, Leiden, E.J. Brill.
(18) *The Holy Bible* (n.d.), Cambridge, Cambridge University Press.
(19) Blakney, R.B. (1941), *Meister Eckhart*, New York, Harper & Row.
(20) Bohm, D. (1980), *Wholeness and the Implicate Order*, London, Routledge & Kegan Paul.
(21) Bord, J. and Bord, C. (1982), *Earth Rites*, London, Granada.
(23) Bord, J. and Bord, C. (1978), *The Secret Country*, London, Granada.
(24) Brandon, S.G.F. (1973), *Religion in Ancient History*, London, Allen & Unwin.

(25) Branston, B. (1957), *The Lost Gods of England*, London, Thames & Hudson.
(26) Brennan, M. (1983), *The Stars and the Stones*, London, Thames & Hudson.
(27) Brown, P. (1976), *Megaliths, Myths and Men*, Dorset, Blandford Press.
(28) Brown, P. (1980), *The Book of Kells*, London, Thames & Hudson.
(29) Burl, A. (1976), *The Stone Circles of the British Isles*, New Haven, Connecticut, Yale University Press.
(30) Burl, A. (1981), *Rites of the Gods*, London, J.M. Dent.
(31) Burl, A. (1983), *Prehistoric Astronomy and Ritual*, Aylesbury, Shire.
(32) Caesar (1979), *The Conquest of Gaul*, trans. J. Gardner after S.A. Handford, Harmondsworth, Penguin.
(33) Campbell, J. (1968), *Creative Mythology (Masks of God)*, London, Secker & Warburg.
(34) Campbell, J. (1976a), *Occidental Mythology (Masks of God)*, Hardmondsworth, Penguin.
(35) Campbell, J. (1976b), *Primitive Mythology (Masks of God)*, Harmondsworth, Penguin.
(36) Campbell, J. (1984), *The Way of the Animal Powers*, London, Times Books.
(37) Campbell, J. (1985), *Myths To Live By*, London, Granada.
(38) Carmichael, A. (1960), *The Sun Dances*, London, Christian Community Press.
(39) Carylon, R. (1981), *Guide to the Gods*, London, Heinemann.
(40) Ceram, C.W. (1967), *Gods, Graves and Scholars*, Harmondsworth, Penguin.
(41) Chadwick, N. (1970), *The Celts*, Hardmondsworth, Penguin.
(42) Childe, G. (1942), *What Happened In History*, Harmondsworth, Penguin.
(43) Childe, G. (1957), *The Dawn of European Civilisation*, New York, Granada.
(44) Chrétien de Troyes (1914), *Arthurian Romances*, trans. W.W. Comfort, London, J.M. Dent.
(45) Cicero (1980), *Selected Works*, trans. M. Grant, Harmondsworth, Penguin.
(46) Clark, G. and Piggott, S. (1970), *Prehistoric Societies*, Harmondsworth, Penguin.
(47) Craighead, M. (1979), *The Sign of the Tree*, London, Mitchell Beazley.
(48) Craighead, M. (1982), 'Immanent Mother', in Giles, M.E. (ed.), *The Feminist Mystic*, New York, Crossroad.
(49) Crawford, O.G.S. (1957), *The Eye Goddess*, London, Phoenix House.

(50) Dames, M. (1980), *The Avebury Cycle*, London, Thames & Hudson.
(51) Dames, M. (1981), *The Silbury Treasure*, London, Thames & Hudson.
(52) Darrah, J. (1981), *The Real Camelot*, London, Thames & Hudson.
(53) Davidson, H.R.E. (1964), *Gods and Myths of Northern Europe*, Harmondsworth, Penguin.
(54) Diodorus Siculus (1939), trans. Oldfather, C.H., London, Heinemann.
(55) Drury, N. (1978), *The Shaman and the Magician*. London, Routledge & Kegan Paul.
(56) Duckett, E. (1959), *The Wandering Saints*, London, Collins.
(57) Eliade, M. (1958), *Patterns in Comparative Religion*, London, Sheed & Ward.
(58) Eliade, M. (1960), *Myths, Dreams and Mysteries*, London, Harvill Press.
(59) Eliade, M. (1961), *Images and Symbols*, London, Harvill Press.
(60) Eliade, M. (1962), *The Forge and the Crucible*, London, Rider & Co.
(61) Eliade, M. (1964a), *Myth and Reality*, London, Allen & Unwin.
(62) Eliade, M. (1964b), *Shamanism*, Princeton, New Jersey, Princeton University Press.
(63) Eliade, M. (1974), *The Myth of the Eternal Return*, Princeton, New Jersey, Princeton University Press.
(64) Eliade, M. (1975), *The Quest*, Chicago, University of Chicago Press.
(65) Eliade, M. (1979), *History of Religious Ideas, Vol. I*, London, Collins.
(66) Ferguson, J. (1970), *The Religions of the Roman Empire*, London, Thames & Hudson.
(67) Fowler, P. (1967), *Wessex*, London, Heinemann.
(68) Fowles, J. and Brukoff, B. (1980), *The Enigma of Stonehenge*, London, Jonathan Cape.
(69) Geoffrey of Monmouth (1966), *Historia Regum Brittania*, trans. L. Thorp, Harmondsworth, Penguin.
(70) Gimbutas, M. (1974), *The Goddesses and Gods of Old Europe*, London, Thames & Hudson.
(71) Godwin, J. (1981), *Mystery Religions and the Ancient World*, London, Thames & Hudson.
(72) Govinda, Lama A. (1960), *Foundations of Tibetan Mysticism*, London, Rider & Co.
(73) Graves, R. (1958), *The Greek Myths*, London, Cassell & Co.
(74) Graves, R. (1961), *The White Goddess*, London, Faber & Faber.
(75) Graves, T. (1978), *Needles of Stone*, Wellingborough, Turnstone Books.
(76) Green, M.J. (1983), *The Gods of Roman Britain*, Aylesbury, Shire.

(77) Hadingham, E. (1974), *Ancient Carvings in Britain*, London, Garnstone Press.
(78) Hadingham, E. (1975), *Circles and Standing Stones*, London, Heinemann.
(79) Hadingham, E. (1980), *Secrets of the Ice Age*, London, Heinemann.
(80) Halifax, J. (1982), *Shaman: The Wounded Healer*, London, Thames & Hudson.
(81) Hall, M.P. (1935), *The Secret Teachings Of All Ages*, Wellingborough, Thorsons.
(82) Harding, E. (1971), *Women's Mysteries*, London, Rider & Co.
(83) Harner, M. (1980), *The Way of the Shaman*, New York, Harper & Row.
(84) Hartley, C. (1968), *Western Mystery Tradition*, London, Aquarian Press.
(85) Hawkes, J. (1963), *Man and the Sun*, London, Cresset Press.
(86) Hawkins, G.S. (1966), *Stonehenge Decoded*, London, Souvenir Press.
(87) Hitching, F. (1976), *Earth Magic*, London, Cassell & Co.
(88) Hollander, L.M. (1947) *The Skalds*, New York, American-Scandinavian Foundation.
(89) Horton, A. (1975), *The Child Jesus*, New York, Dial Press.
(90) Howard, M. (1978), *The Runes*, Wellingborough, Aquarian Press.
(91) Howard, M. (1980), *The Magic of the Runes*, Wellingborough, Aquarian Press.
(92) Hoyle, F. (1977), *On Stonehenge*, London, Heinemann.
(93) Hughes, K. and Hamlin, A. (1981), *Celtic Monasticism*, New York, Seabury Press.
(94) Jackson, K.H. (trans. and ed.) (1951) *A Celtic Miscellany*, London, Routledge & Kegan Paul.
(95) Jones, R. (1909), *Studies in Mystical Religion*, London, Macmillan & Co.
(96) Kelsey, M.T. (1976), *The Other Side of Silence*, New York, Paulist Press.
(98) Kerenyi, C. (1951), *Gods of the Greeks*, London, Thames & Hudson.
(99) Knight, G. (1983), *The Secret Tradition in Arthurian Legend*, Wellingborough, Aquarian Press.
(100) Kühn, H. (1958), *On the Track of Prehistoric Man*, London, Arrow Books.
(101) Kühn, H. (1966), *The Rock Pictures of Europe*, London, Sidgwick & Jackson.
(102) Laing, L. (1981), *Celtic Britain*, London, Granada.
(103) Laing, L. and Laing, J. (1980), *The Origins of Britain*, London, Routledge & Kegan Paul.

(104) *Larousse, New Encyclopedia of Mythology* (1969), London, Hamyln.
(105) Lethbridge, T.C. (1967), *Witches*, London, Jonathan Cape.
(106) Lévi-Strauss, C. (1965), *Structural Anthropology, Vol. I*, trans. Jacobsen, C. and Schoepf, B.G., Harmondsworth, Penguin.
(107) Levy, G. (1948), *The Gate of Horn*, London, Faber & Faber.
(108) Lissnar, I. (1961), *Man, God and Magic*, London, Jonathan Cape.
(109) Lissnar, I. (1963), *The Silent Past*, London, Jonathan Cape.
(110) *Mabinogion* Vols. I and II (n.d.) trans. Lady C. Guest, London, Longman, Brown and Green.
(111) MacCana, P. (1970), *Celtic Mythology*, London, Hamlyn.
(112) MacKie, E. (1977), *Science and Society in Prehistoric Britain*, London, Granada.
(113) Malinowski, B. (1948), *Magic, Science and Religion and Other Essays*, New York, Free Press.
(114) Maringer, J. (1960), *The Gods of Prehistoric Man*, London, Weidenfeld & Nicolson.
(115) Markale, J. (1978), *Celtic Civilisation*, London, Gordon & Cremonesi.
(116) Marshack, A. (1972), *The Roots of Civilisation*, London, Weidenfeld & Nicolson.
(117) Massingham, H.J. (1926), *Downland Man*, London, Jonathan Cape.
(118) Matthews, C. and Matthews, J. (1985), *The Western Way*, London, Routledge & Kegan Paul.
(119) Merton, T. (1961a), *Mystics and Zen Masters*, New York, Dell.
(120) Merton, T. (1961b), *The Wisdom of the Desert*, London, Hollis & Carter.
(121) Meyer, K. and Nutt, A. (1895), *The Voyage of Bran, Son of Febal*, London, David Nutt.
(122) Michell, J. (1975), *The Earth Spirit*, London, Thames & Hudson.
(123) Murdoch, I. (1983), *The Philosopher's Pupil*, London, Chatto & Windus.
(124) Murray, M. (1963), *The Genesis of Religion*, London, Routledge & Kegan Paul.
(125) Murray, M. (n.d.), *The God of the Witches*, London, Sampson Low, Marston & Co.
(126) Needleman, J. (1983), *The Heart of Philosophy*, London, Routledge & Kegan Paul.
(127) Neumann, E. (1954), *The Great Mother*, Princeton, New Jersey, Princeton University Press.
(128) O'Rahilly, T.F. (1946), *Early Irish History and Mythology*, Dublin, Dublin Institute of Advanced Studies.
(129) Otto, R. (1923), *The Idea of the Holy*, Oxford, Oxford University Press.

(130) Paturi, F. (1979), *Prehistoric Heritage*, London, Macdonald & Jane's.

(131) Pearce, R.T. (1982), *Stones, Bones and Gods*, London, Ward Lock.

(132) Perera, S.B. (1981), *Descent to the Goddess*, Toronto, Inner City Books.

(133) Perry, W.J. (1937), *The Growth of Civilisation*, Harmondsworth, Penguin.

(134) Phillips, G.R. (1976), *Brigantia*, London, Routledge & Kegan Paul.

(135) Phillips, P. (1980), *The Prehistory of Europe*, Harmondsworth, Penguin.

(136) Piggott, S. (1954), *Neolithic Culture of the British Isles*, Cambridge, Cambridge University Press.

(137) Piggott, S. (1968), *The Druids*, London, Thames & Hudson.

(138) Plutarch (1952), *Moralia VI*, trans. Babitt, F.R., London, Heinemann.

(139) Powell, T.G.E. (1980), *The Celts*, London, Thames & Hudson.

(140) Rees, A. and Rees, B. (1978), *Celtic Heritage*, London, Thames & Hudson.

(141) Renfrew, C. (1976), *Before Civilisation*, Harmondsworth, Penguin.

(142) Renfrew, C. (1978), *The Megalithic Men of Western Europe*, London, Thames & Hudson.

(143) Richmond, L.A. (1975), *Roman Britain*, Harmondsworth, Penguin.

(144) Robins, D. (1983), 'The Dragon Project', reported S. Thomas, *Guardian*, 25 June.

(145) Robins, D. (1985), *Circles of Silence*, London, Souvenir Press.

(146) Ross, A. (1967), *Pagan Celtic Britain*, London, Routledge & Kegan Paul.

(147) Rutherford, W. (1978), *The Druids*, Wellingborough, Aquarian Press.

(148) Sharkey, J. (1984), *Celtic Mysteries*, London, Thames & Hudson.

(149) Smart, N. (1973), *The Phenomenon of Religion*, New York, Scribner's.

(150) Smart, N. (1977), *The Religious Experience of Mankind*, London, Collins.

(151) Snorri Sturluson. (1929), *The Prose Edda*, New York, American-Scandinavian Foundation.

(152) Squire, C. (1975), *Celtic Myth and Legend*, California, Newcastle.

(153) Steiger, B. (1980), *Worlds Before Our Own*, London, W.H. Allen.

(154) Stern, P. van D. (1979), *Prehistoric Europe*, London, Allen & Unwin.

(155) Tacitus (1970), *The Agricola and the Germania*, Harmondsworth, Penguin.

(156) Tacitus (1948), *Tacitus on Britain and Germany*, trans. Mattingley, H., Harmondsworth, Penguin.
(157) Thom, A. (1967), *Megalithic Sites in Britain*, Oxford, Oxford University Press.
(158) Tolstoy, N. (1985), *The Quest for Merlin*, London, Hamish Hamilton.
(159) Treece, H. (1966), *The Green Man*, London, Bodley Head.
(160) Tremmel, W.C. (1976), *Religion: What Is It?*, New York, Holt, Rinehart & Winston.
(161) Underhill, E. (n.d.(a)), *Mysticism*, London, Methuen.
(162) Underhill, E. (n.d.(b)), *Mystics of the Church*, London, James Clarke & Co.
(163) Warner, M. (1976), *Alone of All Her Sex*, London, Weidenfeld & Nicolson.
(164) Watts, A. (1953), *Myth and Ritual in Christianity*, New York, Vanguard Press.
(165) Watts, A. (1964), *Beyond Theology*, New York, Random House.
(166) Watts, A. (1970), *Does It Matter?*, New York, Random House.
(167) Watts, A. (1972), *The Supreme Identity*, New York, Random House.
(168) Watts, A. (1979), *Tao: The Watercourse Way*, Harmondsworth, Penguin.
(169) Whitelock, D. (1952), *The Beginnings of English Society*, Harmondsworth, Penguin.
(170) Whitmont, E.C. (1983), *Return of the Goddess*, London, Routledge & Kegan Paul.
(171) Wilber, K. (1981), *Up From Eden*, London, Routledge & Kegan Paul.
(172) Wilson, C. (1978), *Mysteries*, London, Hodder & Stoughton.
(173) Wilson, C. (1971), *The Occult*, London, Granada.
(174) Wilson, I. (1984), *Jesus: The Evidence*, London, Weidenfeld and Nicolson.
(175) Wood, J.E., (1978), *Sun, Moon and Standing Stone*, Oxford, Oxford University Press.

Index